Observations of a London Commuter

By
David Fawcett

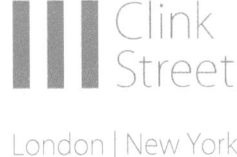

London | New York

Published by Clink Street Publishing 2018

Copyright © 2018

First edition.

The authors assert the moral right under the Copyright, Designs and Patents Act 1988 to be identified as the authors of this work.

All rights reserved. No part of this publication may be reproduced, stored in a retrieval system or transmitted, in any form or by any means without the prior consent of the author, nor be otherwise circulated in any form of binding or cover other than that with which it is published and without a similar condition being imposed on the subsequent purchaser.

ISBN: 978-1-912262-90-8 paperback
978-1-912262-91-5 ebook

Sponsored by
www.depinna.com

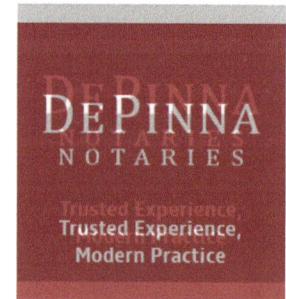

Dedication

With love to Jackie, Tom, Joe and James.

A big thank you to my son Tom for taking the photographs.

David Fawcett is a scrivener notary and partner practising in the firm of De Pinna Notaries in London. As a scrivener notary he specialises in French and Italian notarial work. He has worked in London for thirty years and has commuted from his home in Tunbridge Wells for the last 20 years. He is a self-taught artist and has exhibited widely. Over the years his paintings have formed the subject matter of an album and book cover, music video, a postcard at the Royal Academy and a limited edition range of accessories for Ted Baker.

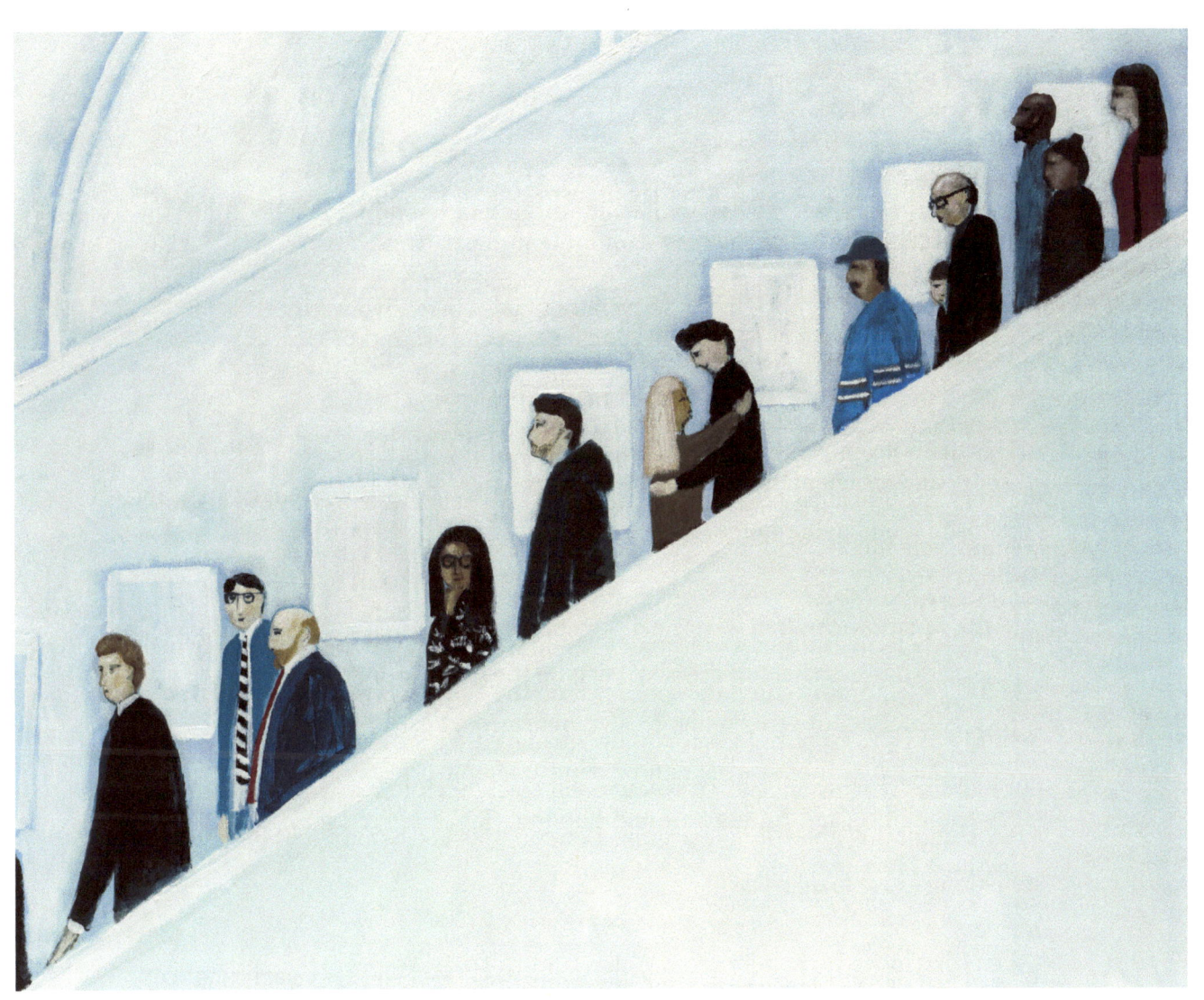

NORMAN MADE A VERY PERCEPTIVE COMMENT ABOUT BREXIT ON THE ESCALATOR

INTRODUCTION

These paintings reflect my day to day life working in London. I live in Tunbridge Wells and have the joy of the daily commute into Charing Cross. I love working in London and enjoy my job as a scrivener notary which involves meetings in the office at Piccadilly and appointments to clients in and around the London area.

I rarely paint from life. In fact the vast majority of my work is based on my visual memory and imagination. My main aim in every painting is to achieve a strong composition and to harmonise the colours as successfully as possible.

Initially when my children were small I would wait until we'd got them off to bed, take a sheet out from behind the sofa, lay it on the living room floor and then start painting. As the years have gone by I've managed to get my own studio sorted out and the living room carpet is now paint free, much to my wife's relief! After a day commuting and running around London, this is where I go to unwind. It's something I love to do.

When I first moved to London from Wales, I did a lot of seascapes as I was brought up in Barry on the coast and missed the sea greatly – I still do! Over time my paintings have become far more reflective of my day to day life. The office environment, commuting and working in London provides a lot of inspiration. Sometimes the subject might be something which strikes me as a good composition like the people grouped around a photocopier trying to sort out a paper jam or tube travellers pressed together on a packed train. Alternatively it might be a subject that just makes me laugh like the naked man working from home or the commuter hiding behind a tree to avoid walking to the station with a tedious fellow commuter (Sad but true - I'm getting quite good at rapid concealment now!). Humour plays a big part in my work. I love trying to convey a situation which makes me laugh.

The title is very important in this and I like trying to find succinct wording to maximise the effect.

This collection of work reflects my working day and the thoughts and feelings it evokes. I hope you enjoy it.

David

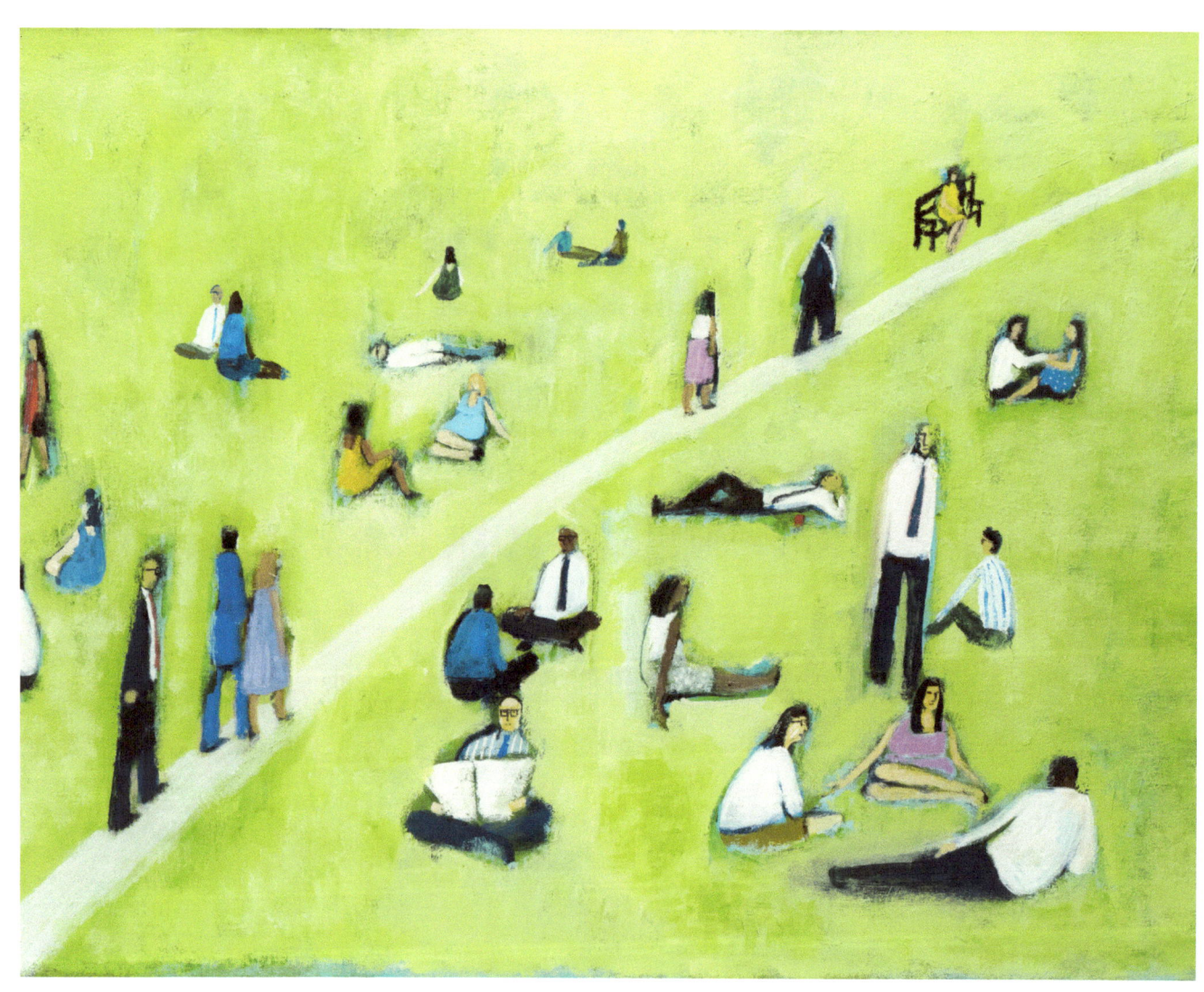

GREEN PARK

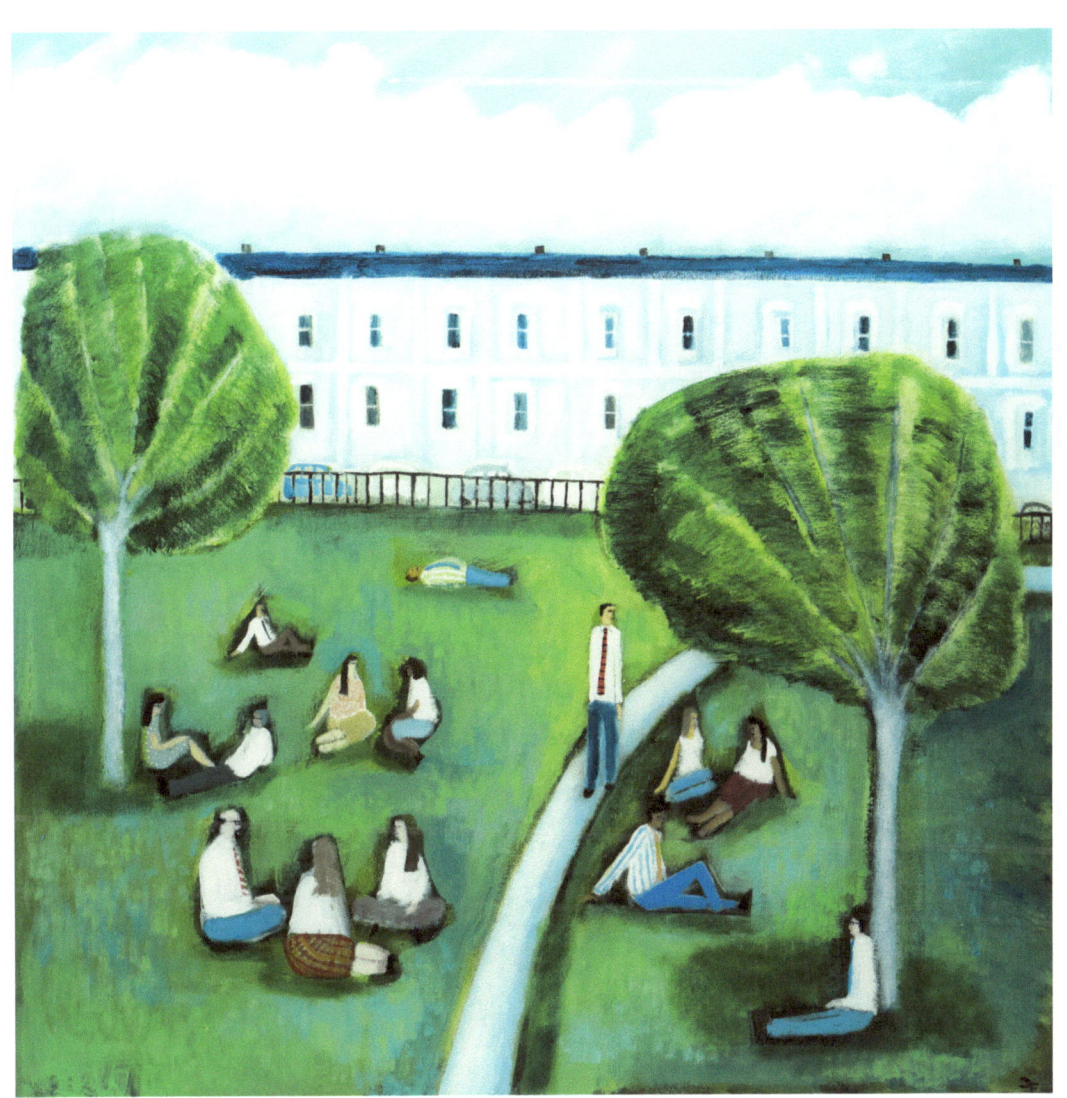

ONE HOUR FOR LUNCH

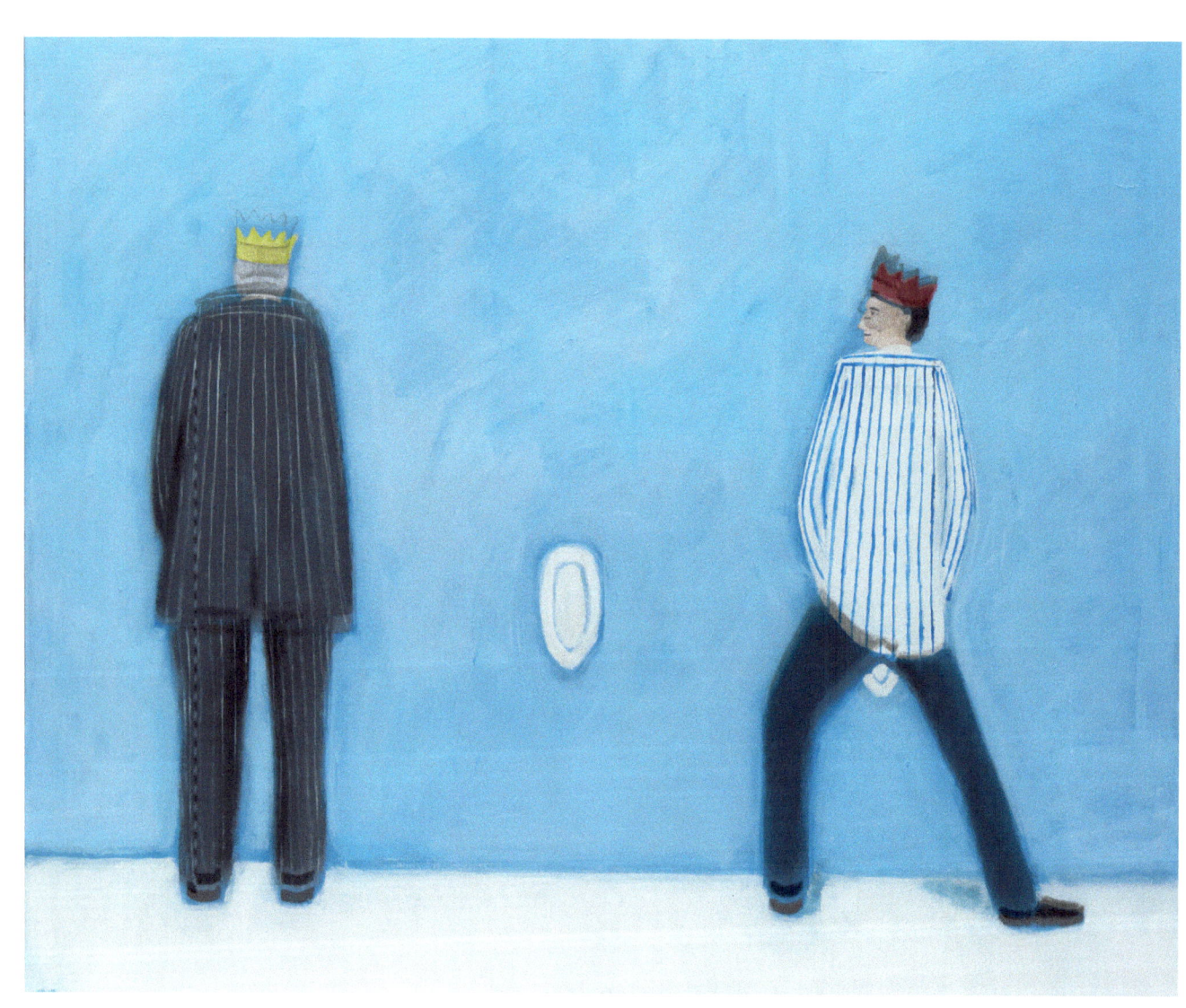

TELLING MY BOSS A FEW HOME TRUTHS

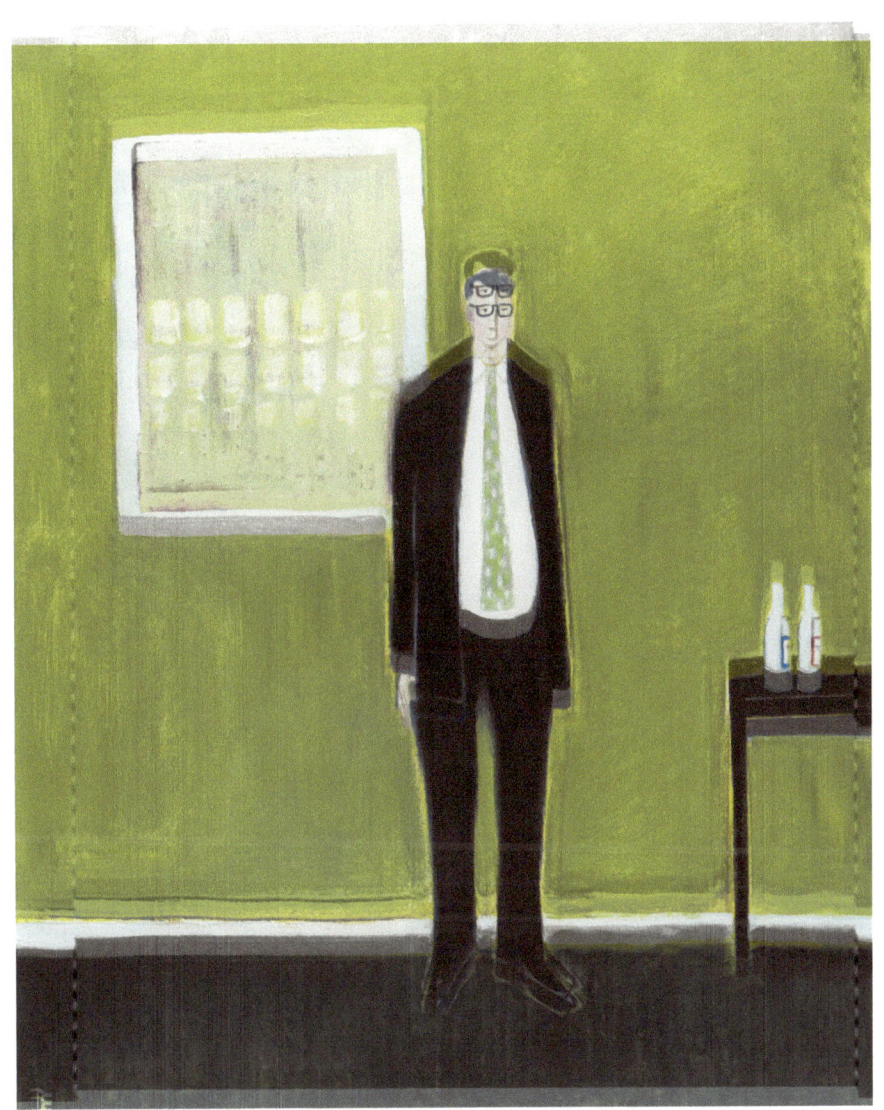

QUIET FART

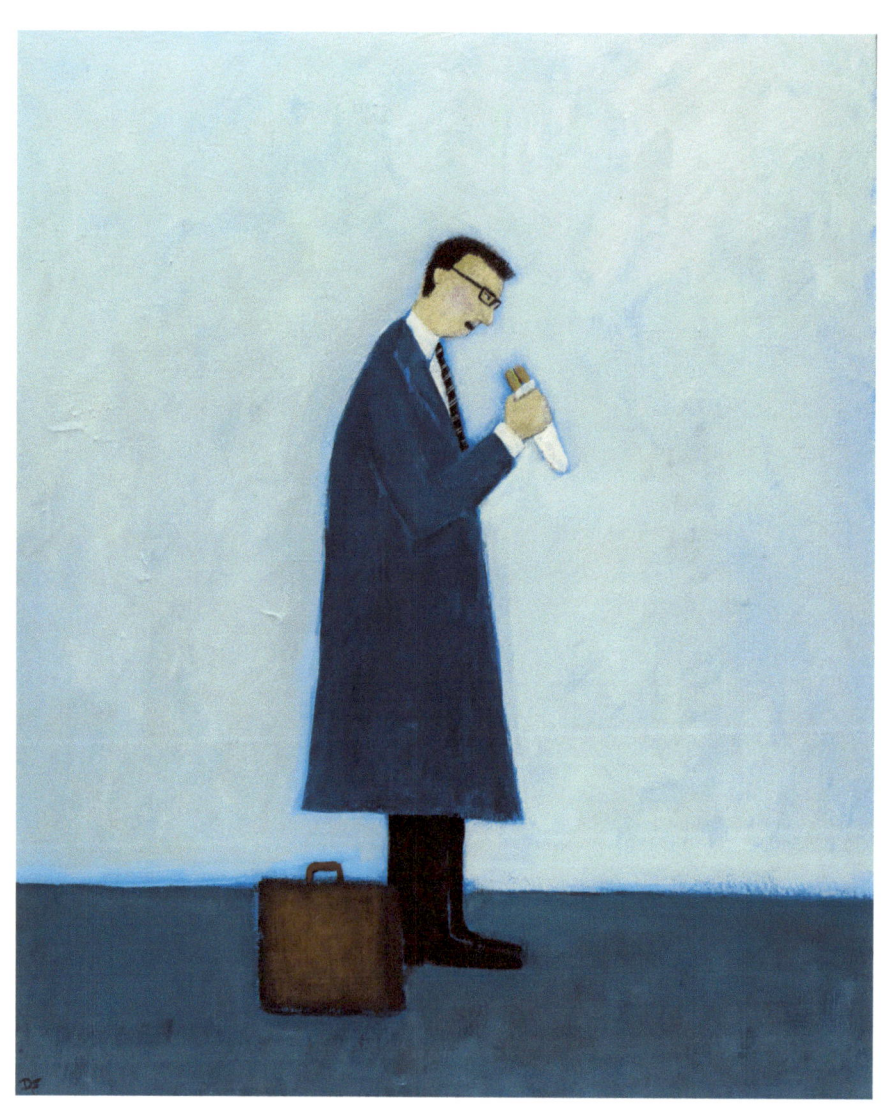

THE DEFENCELESS BAGUETTE

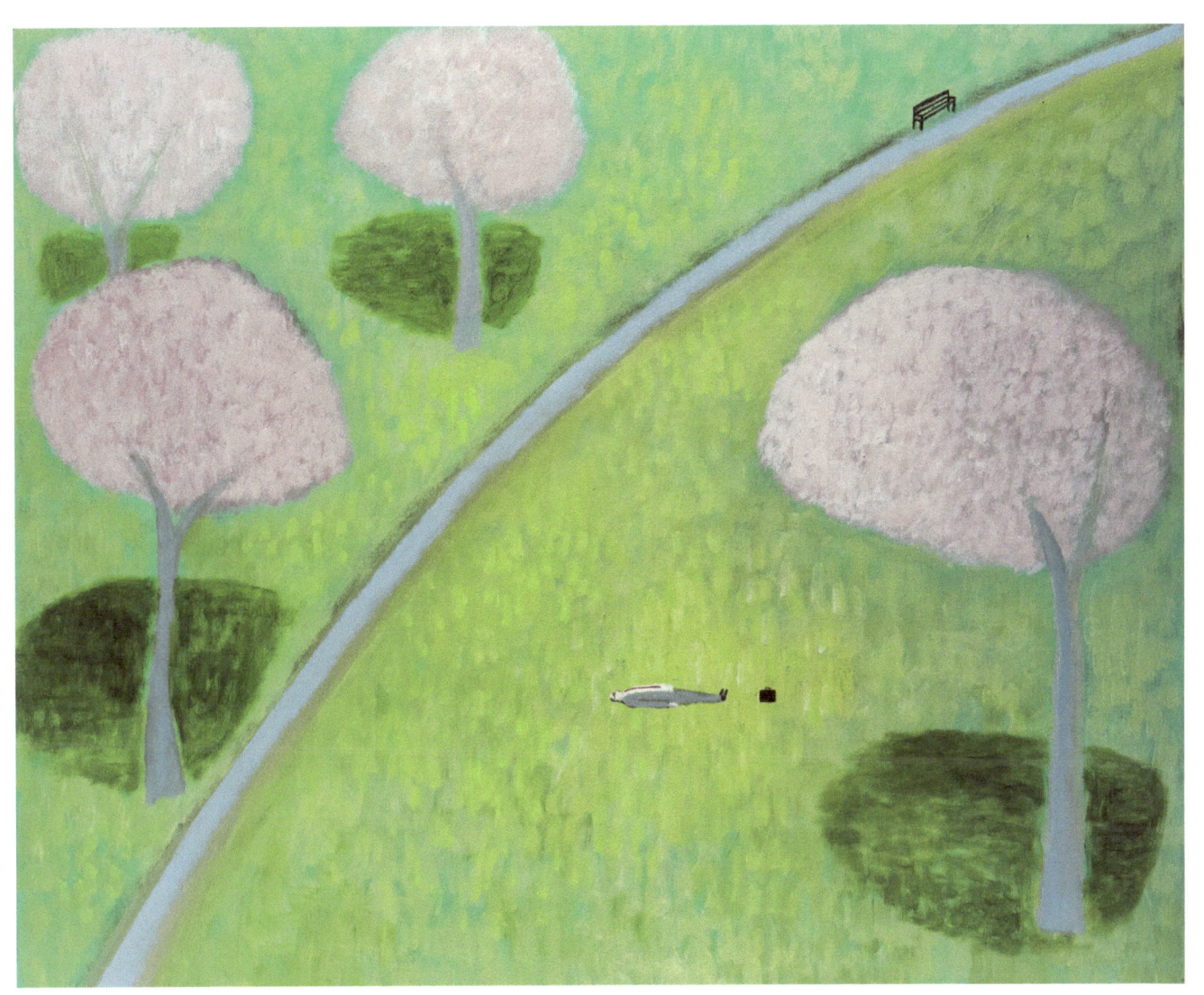

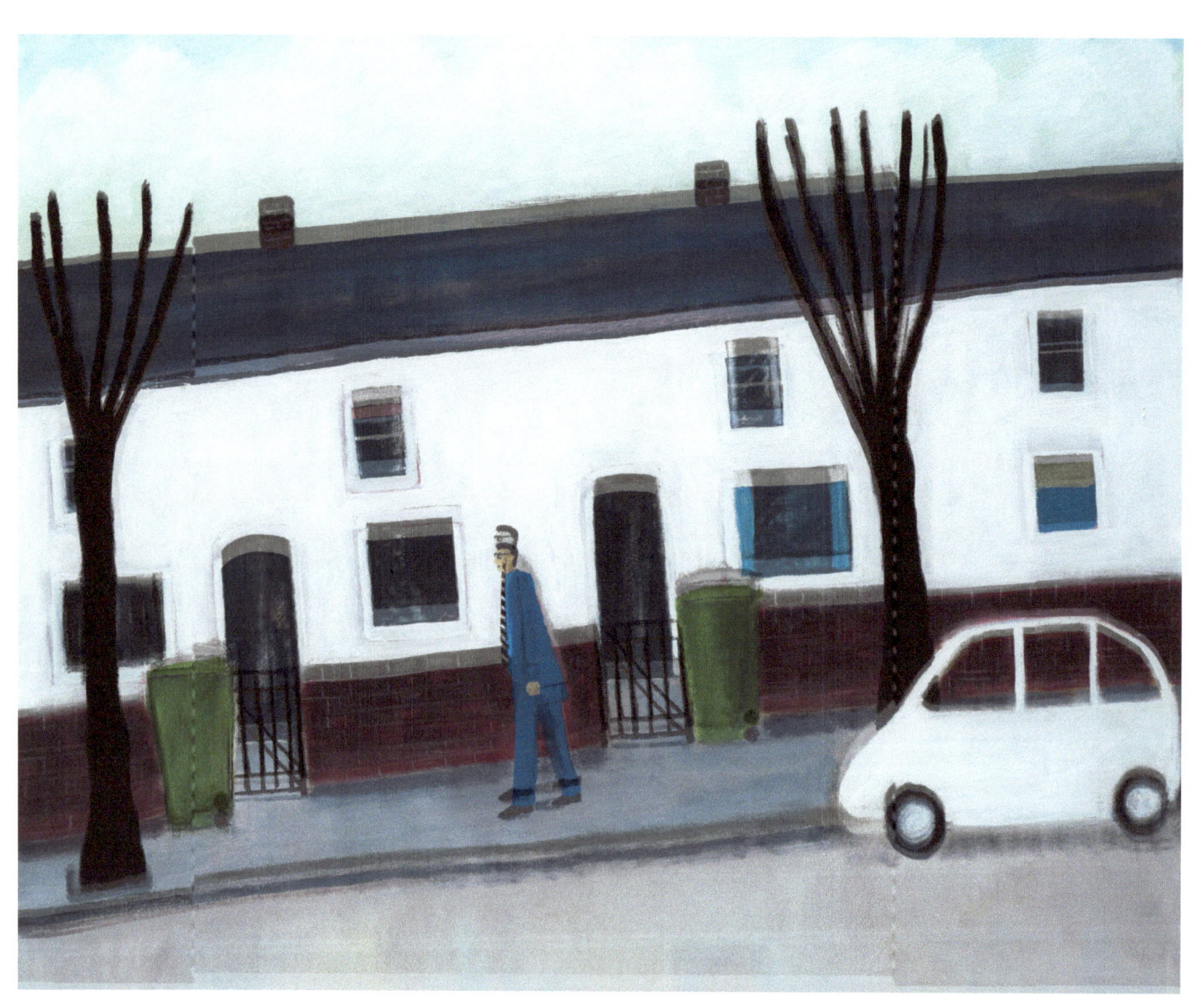

FEELING GOOD IN MY DRY CLEANED SUIT

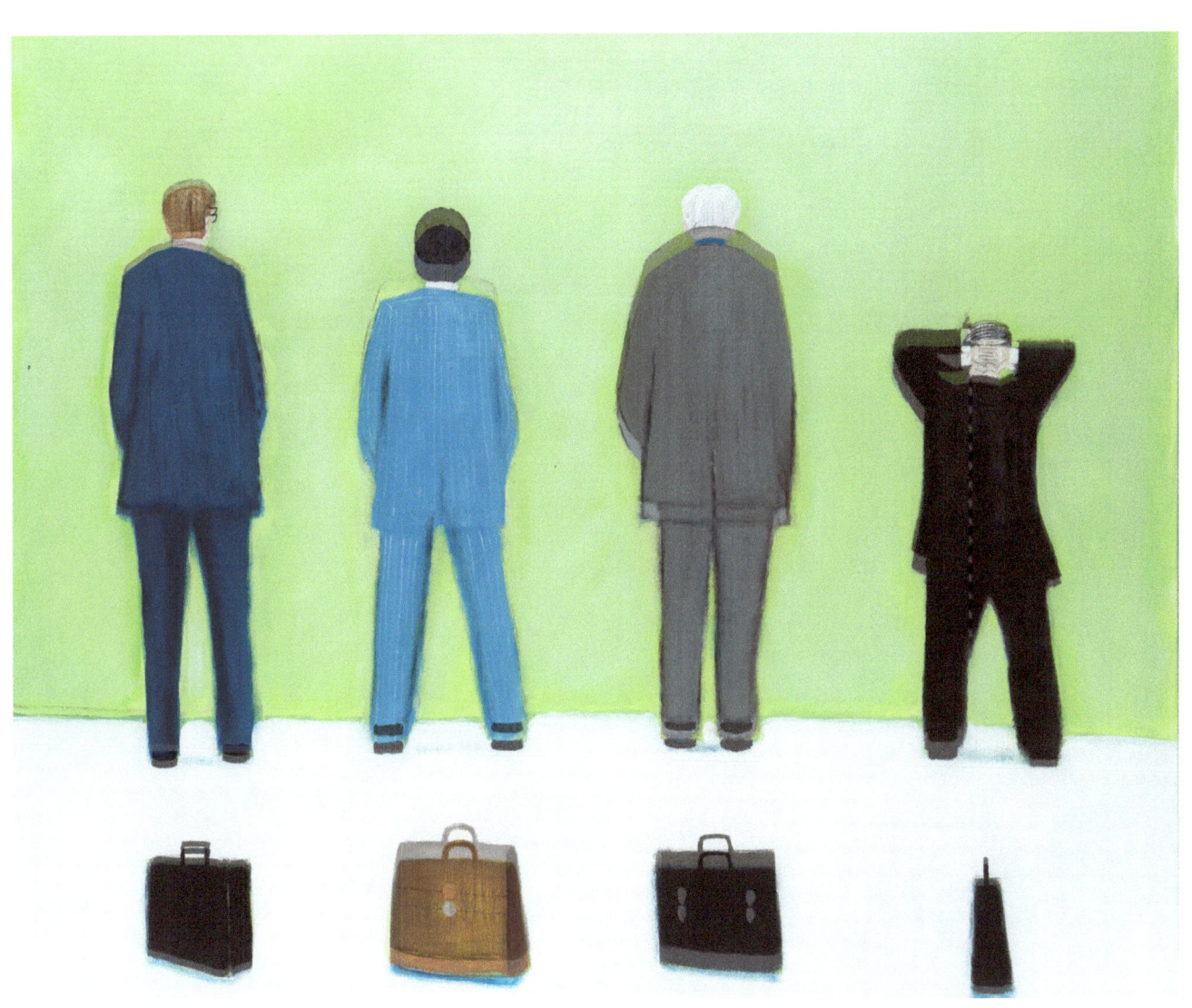

BEFORE THE BIG MEETING

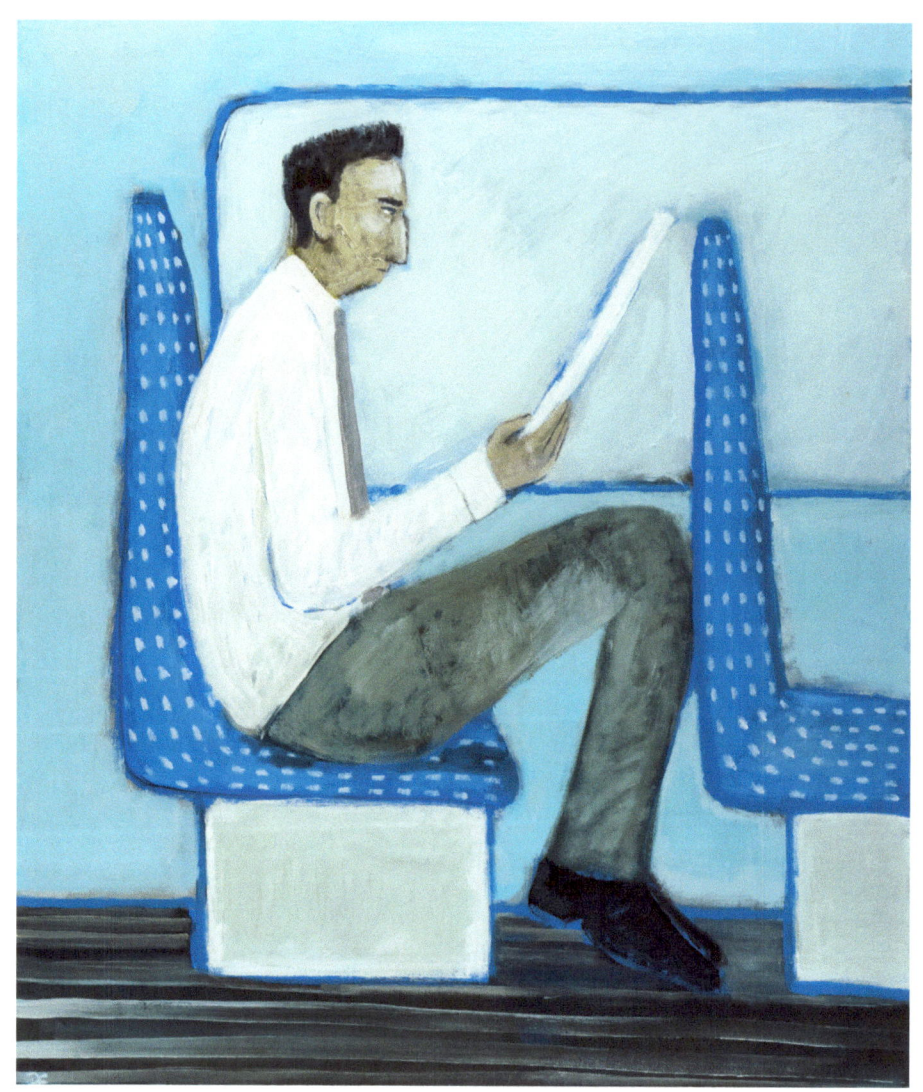

STOP THIS CRUELTY NOW

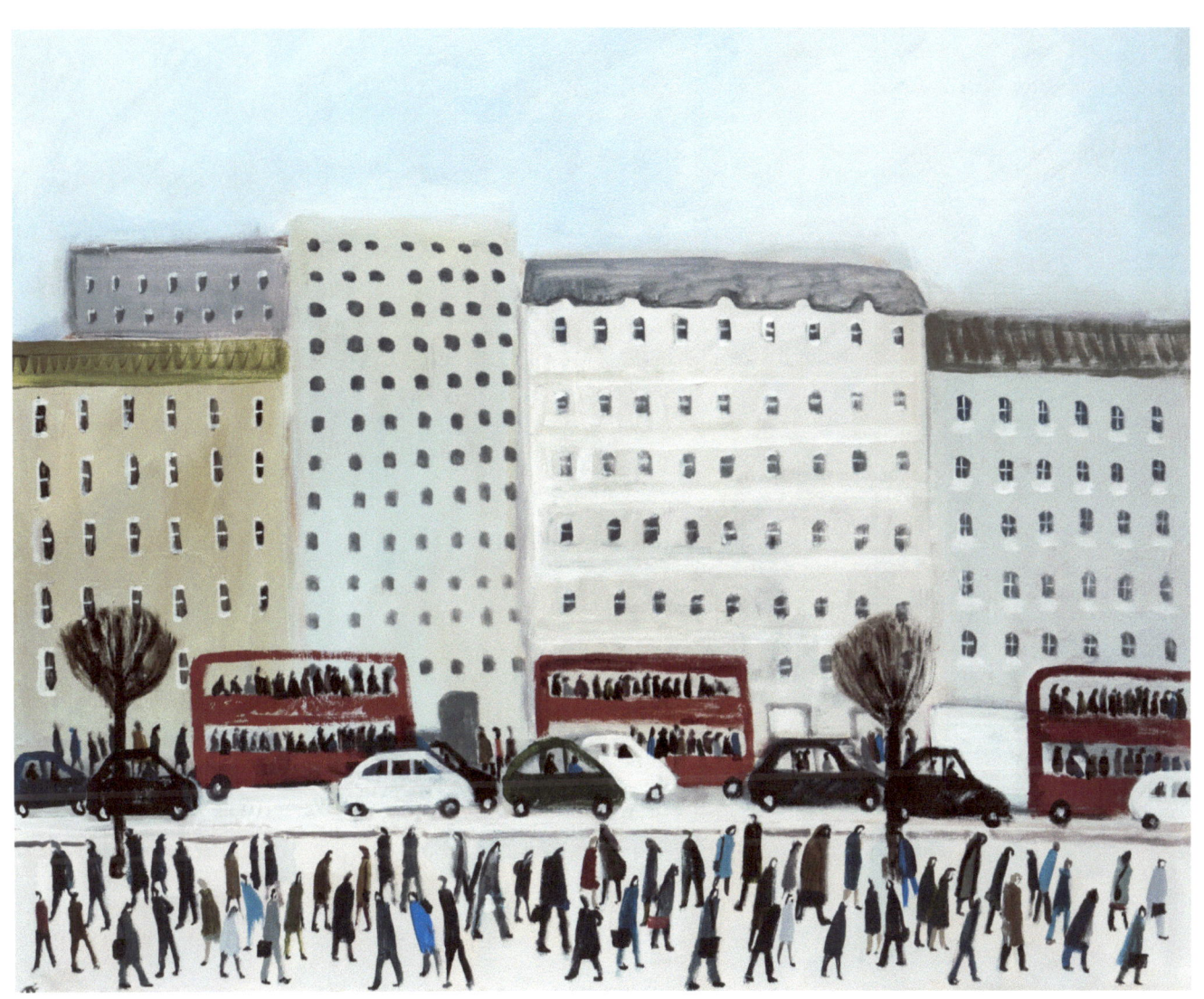

TUBE STRIKE

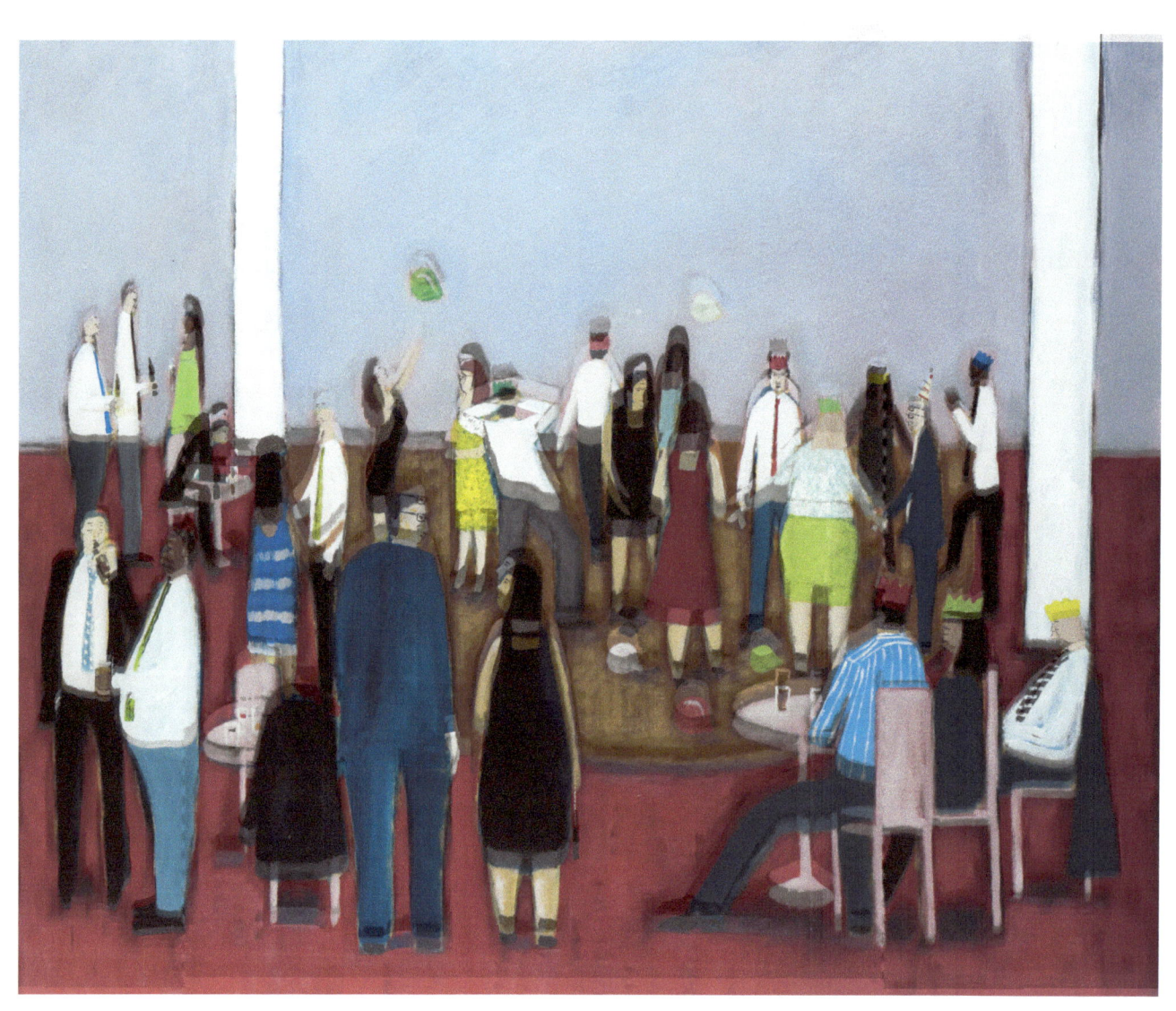

"I WISH DOUGLAS WOULDN'T PERSIST IN DOING THAT DANCE MOVE IN FRONT OF THE SECRETARIES"

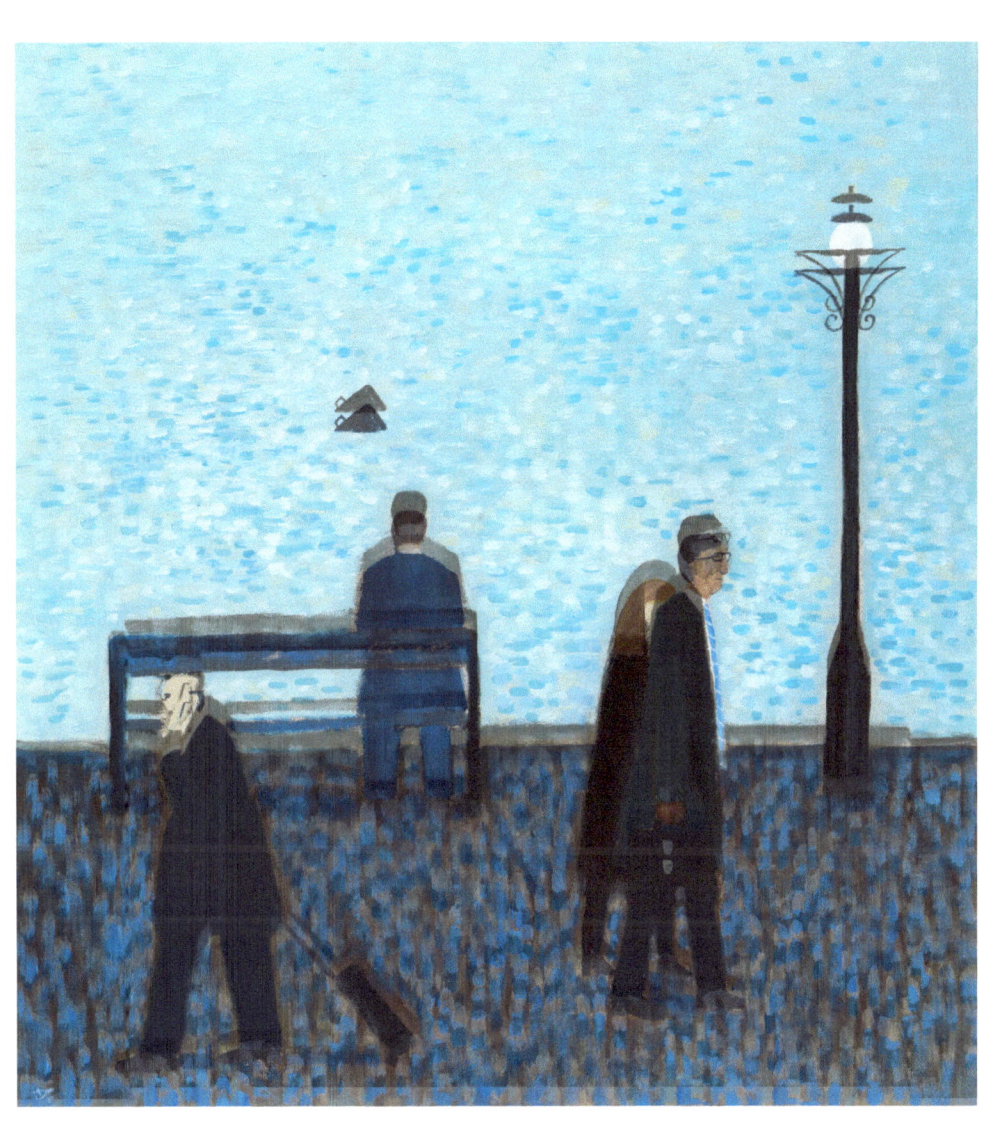

WATCHING MY BRIEF CASE SLOWLY SINK

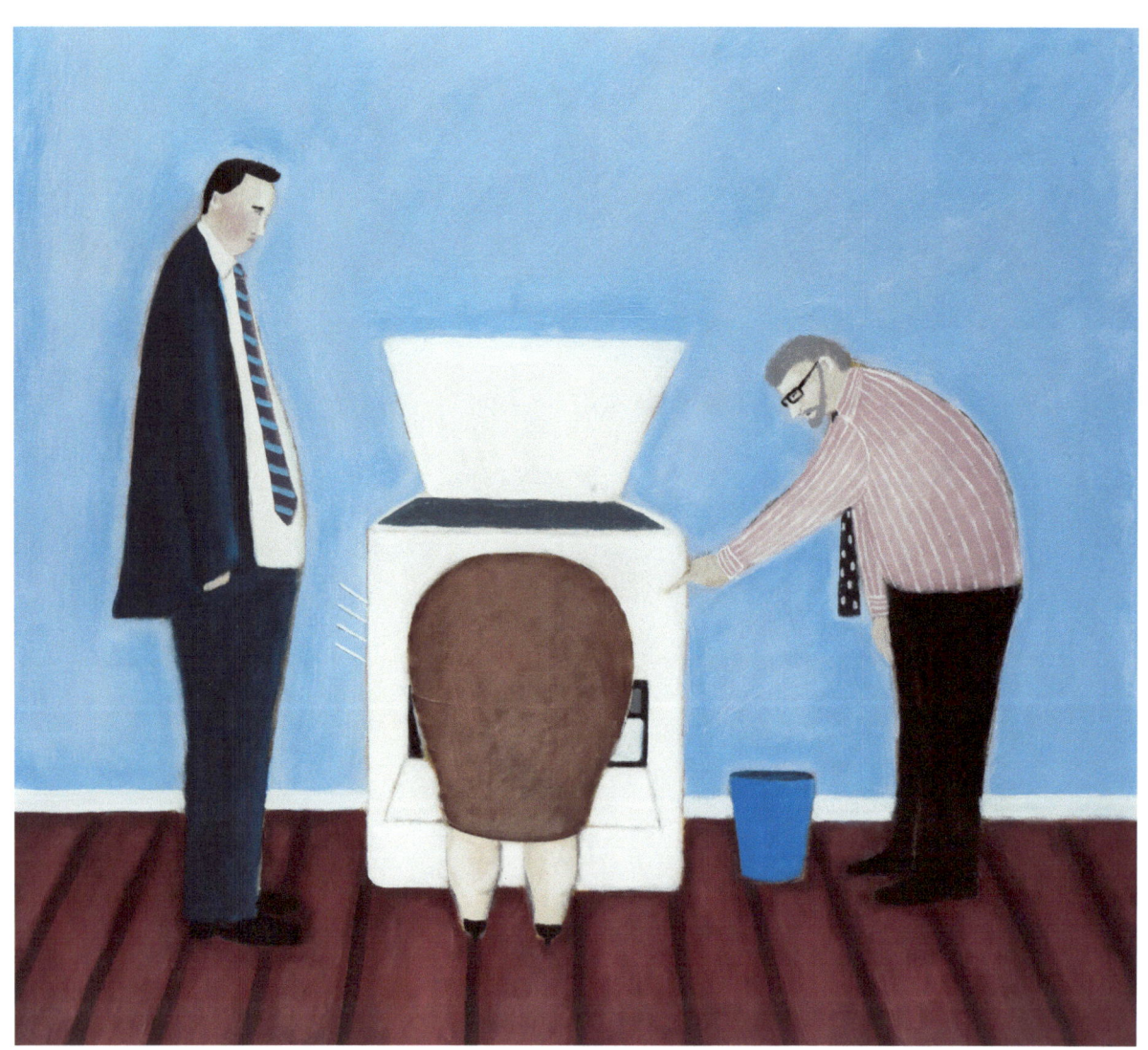

PAPERJAM

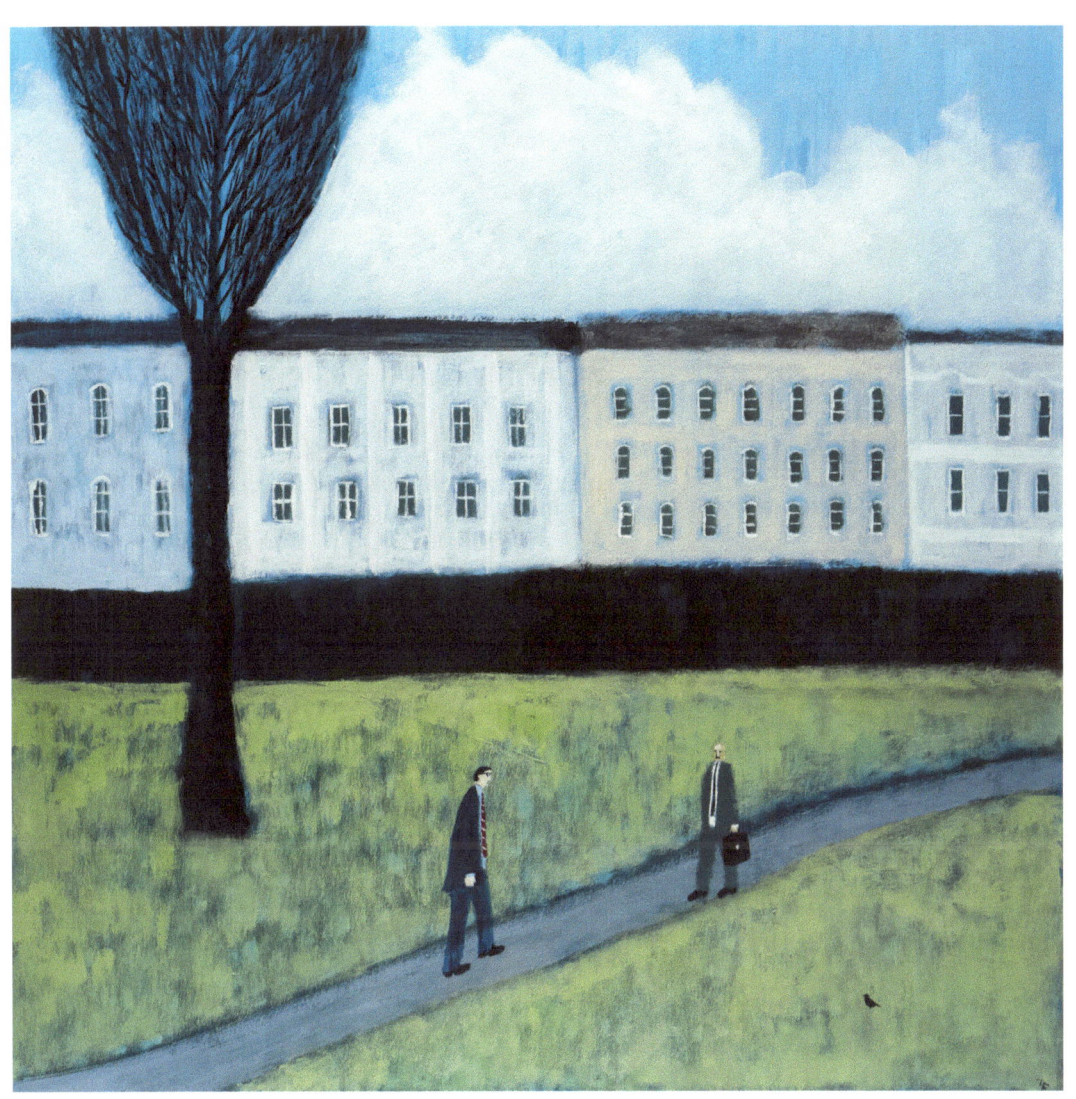

ME AND THE MAN I ALWAYS SAY "MORNING" TO

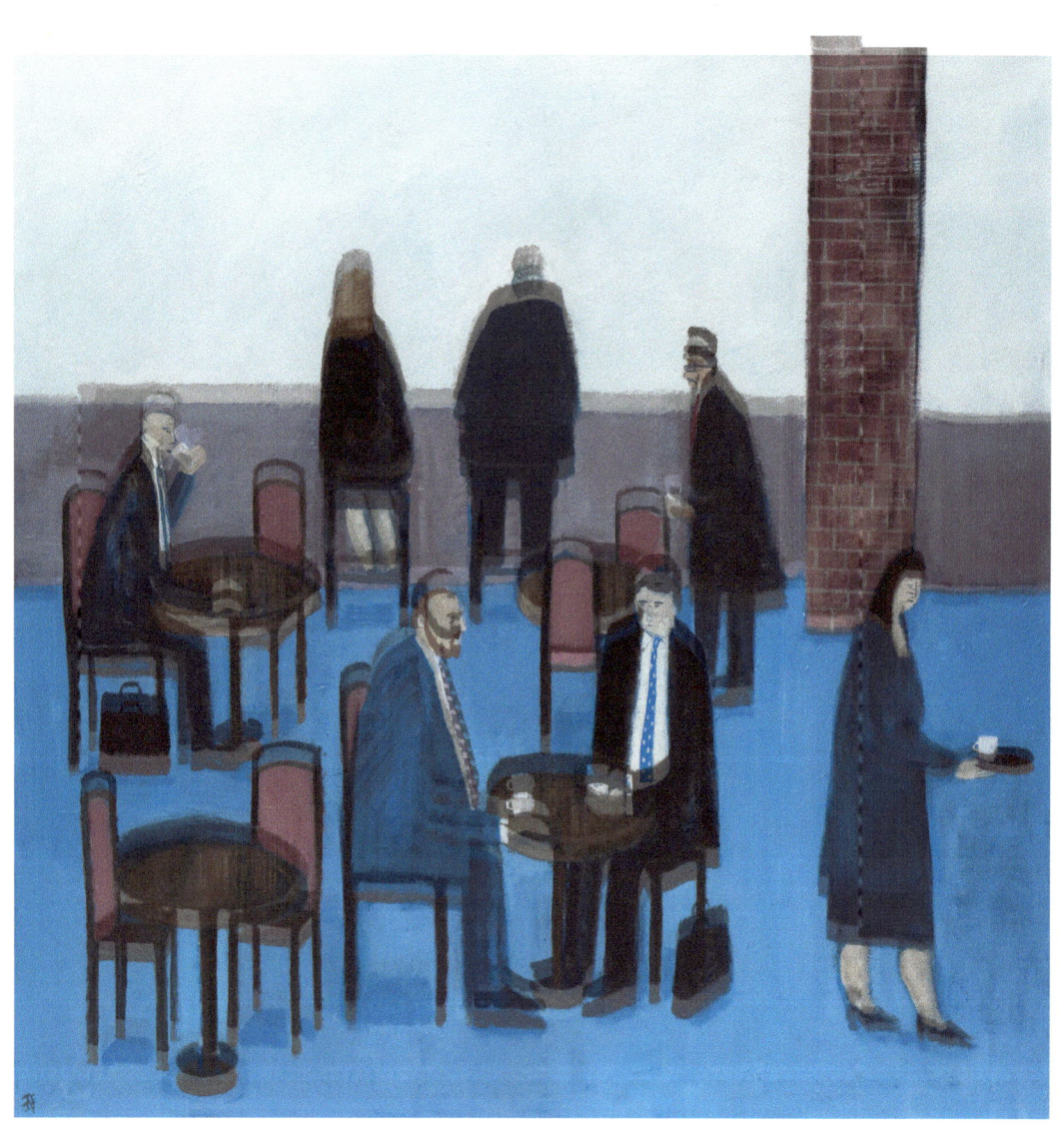

I QUICKLY REALISED THAT JOHN KNOWS ABSOLUTELY NOTHING ABOUT FOOTBALL

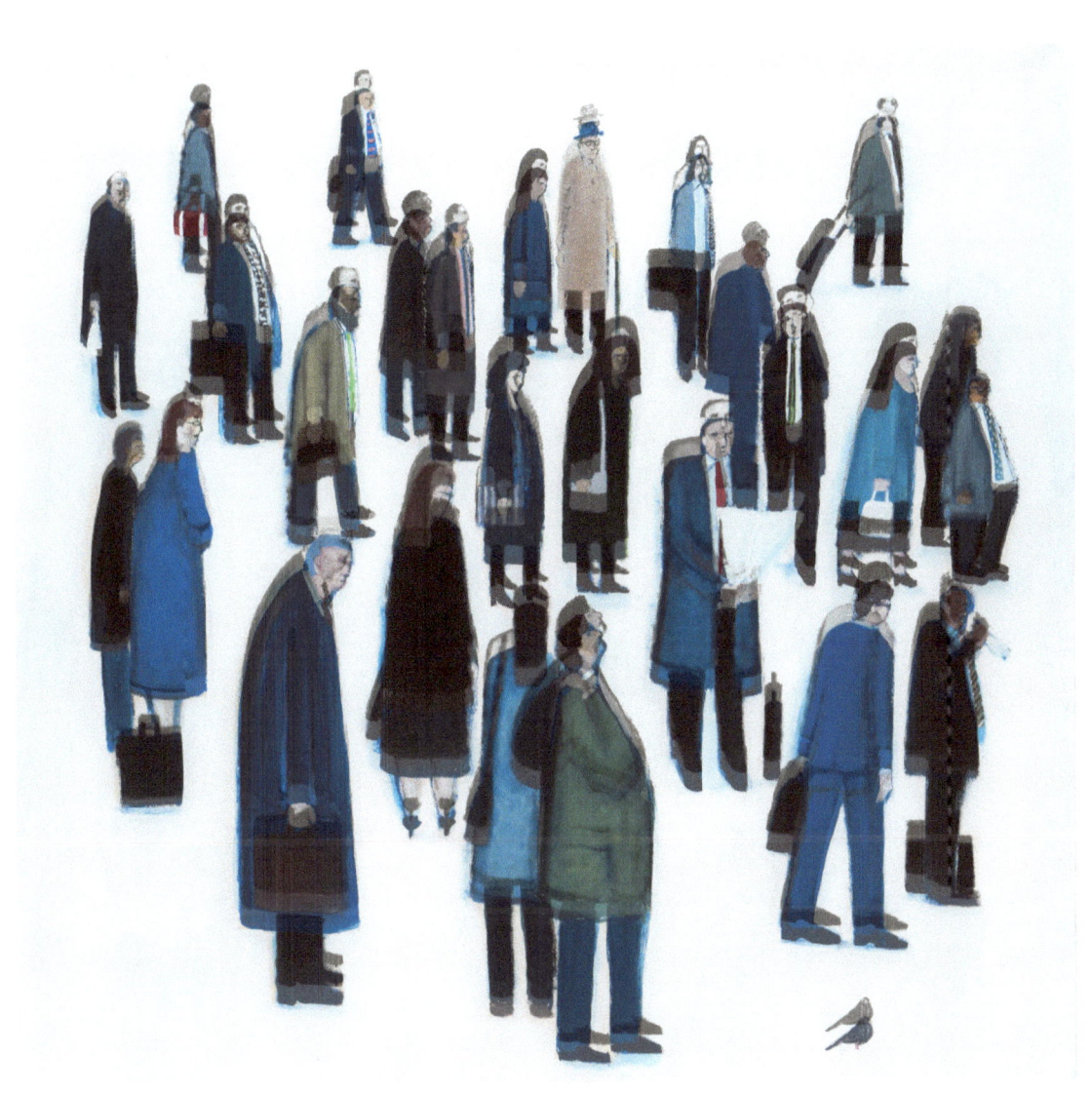

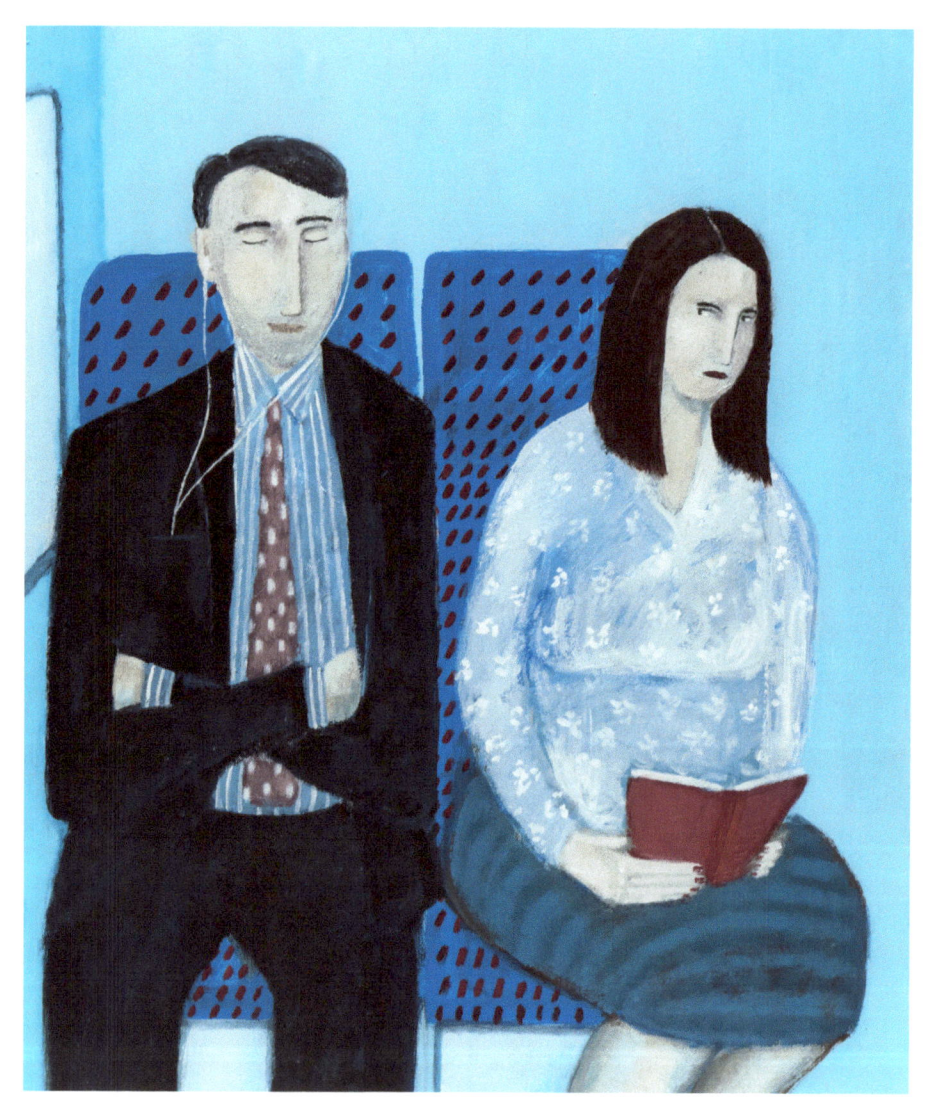

TWO PASSENGERS LISTENING TO STATUS QUO

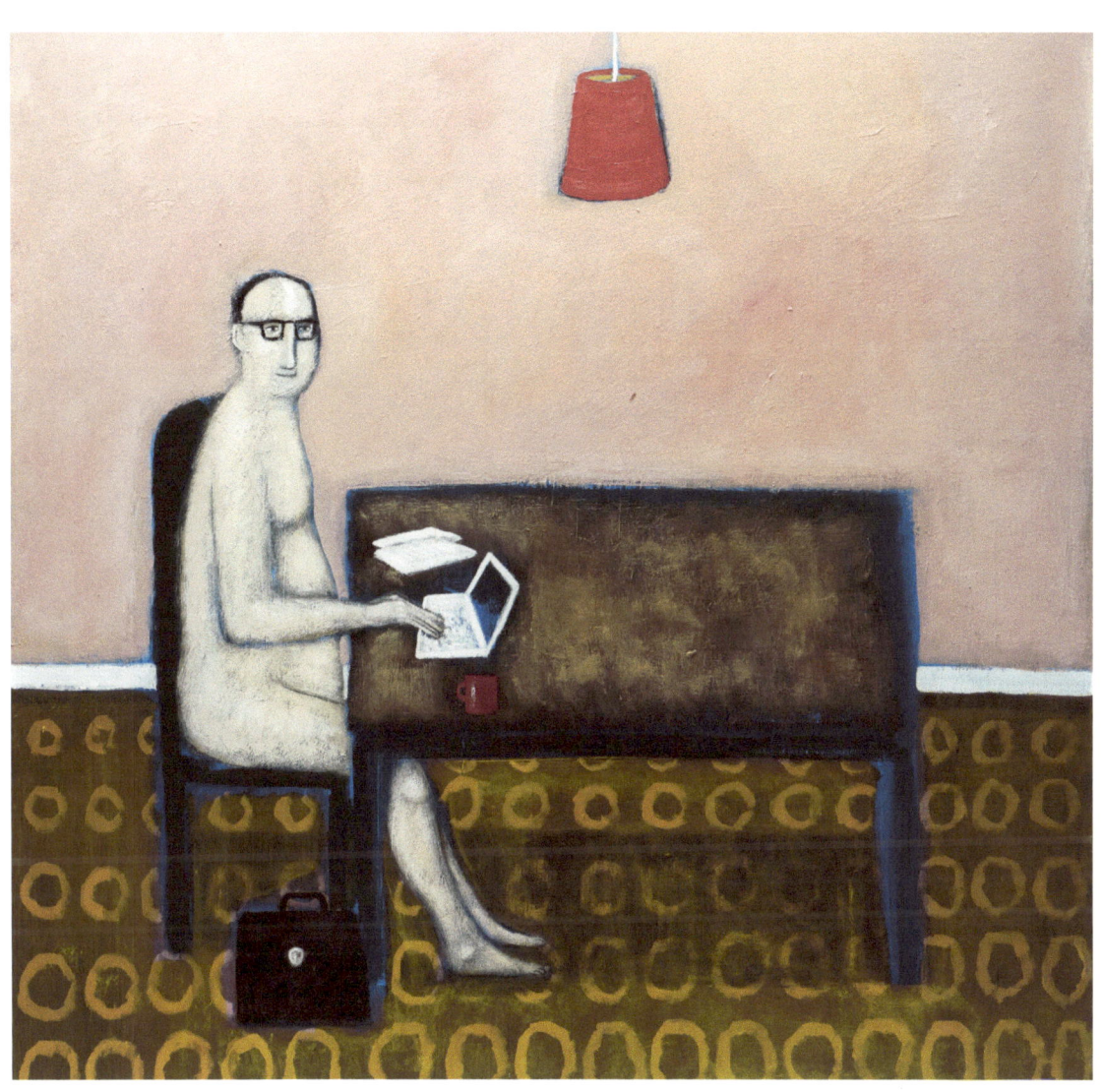

WORKING FROM HOME

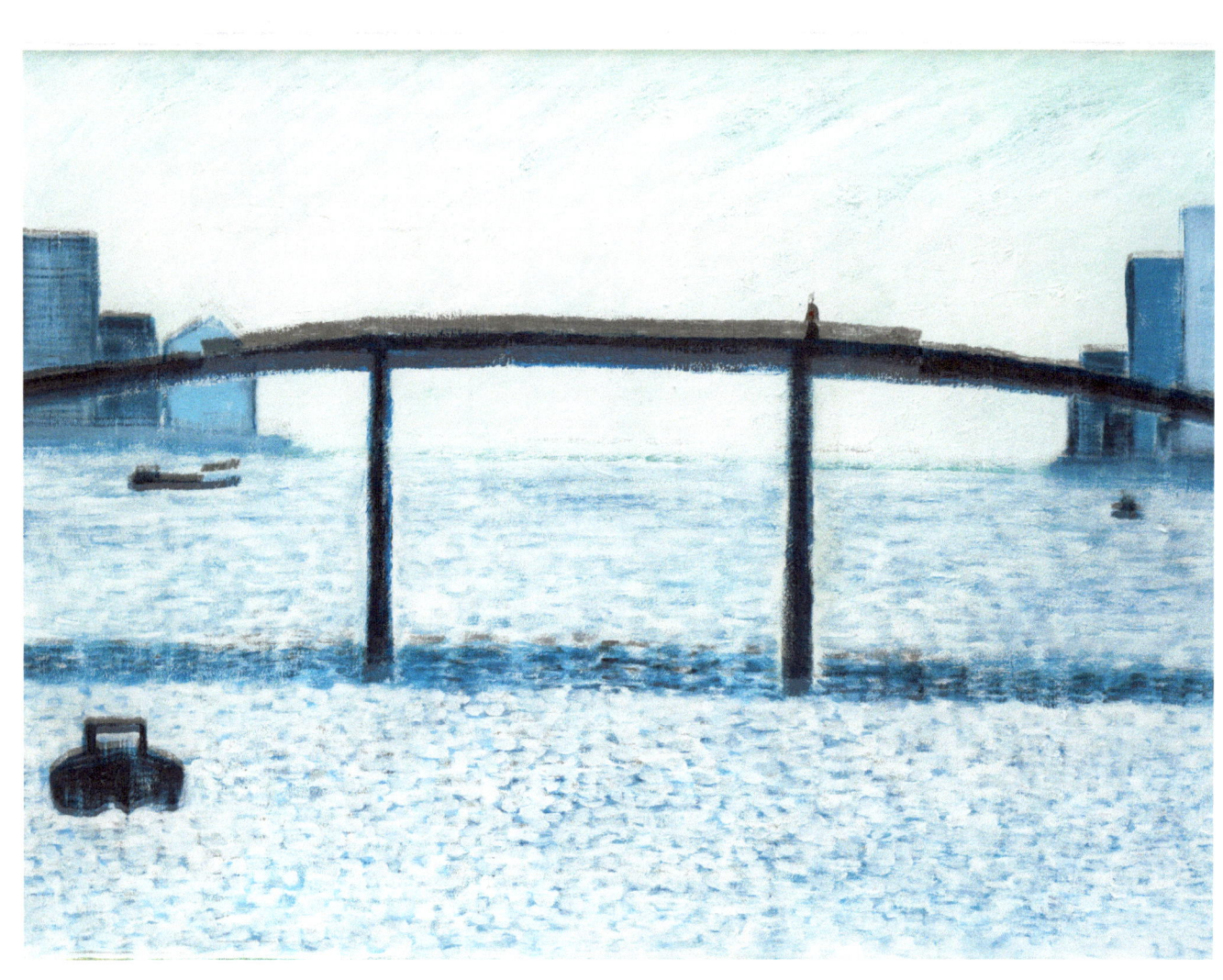

FEELING SELF- CONSCIOUS IN MY NEW BOBBLE HAT

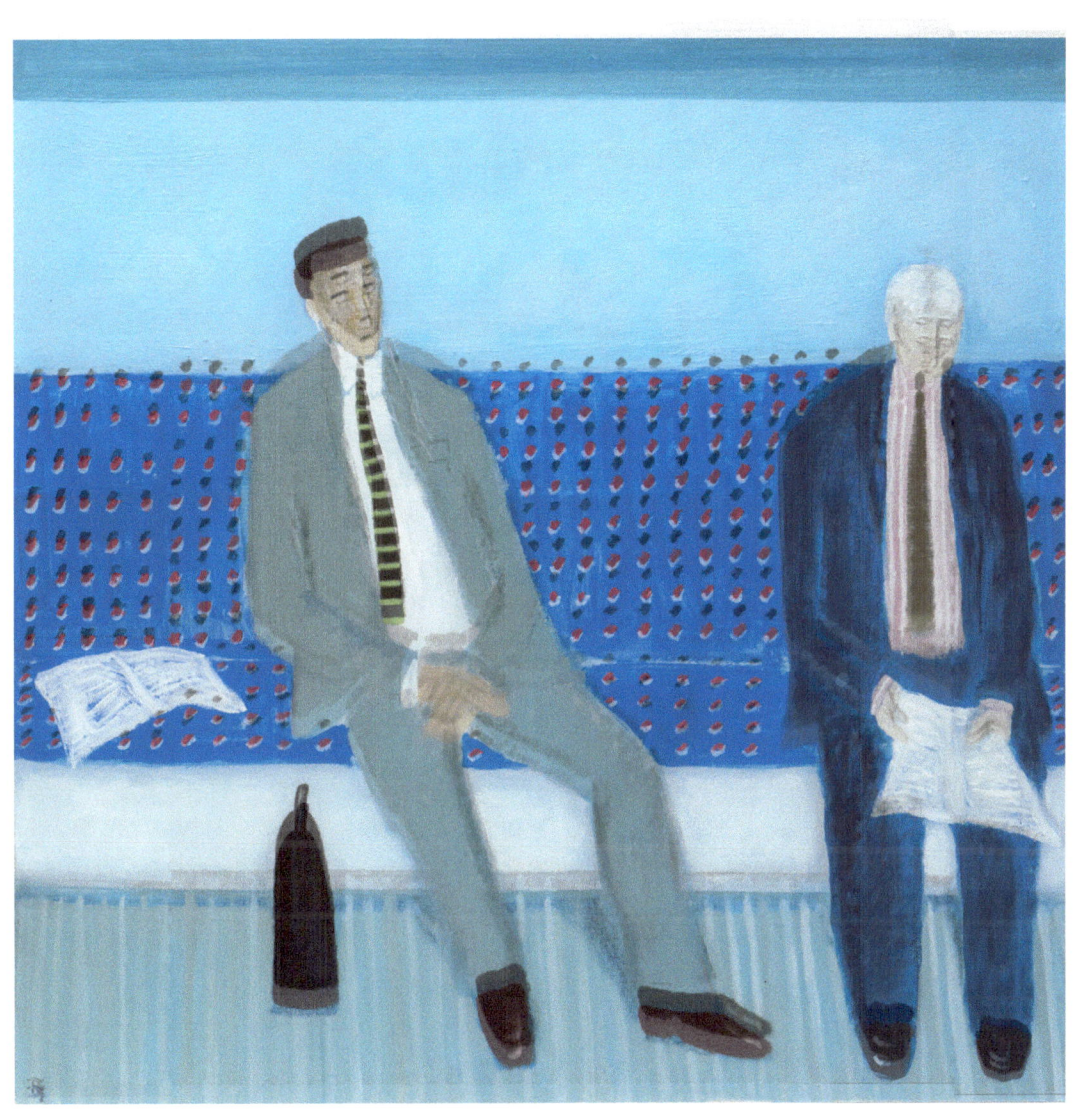

DOZING ON THE DISTRICT LINE

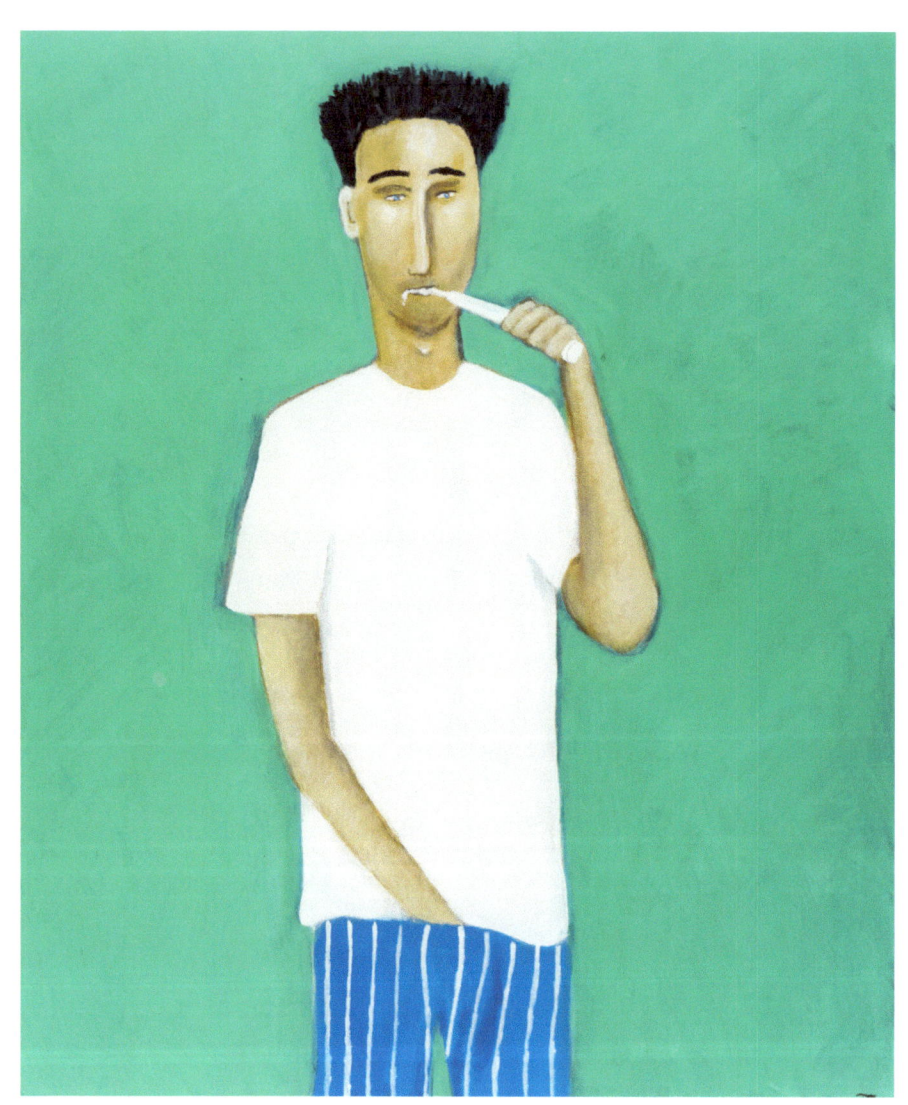

THINKING ABOUT MY LONG TERM FUTURE

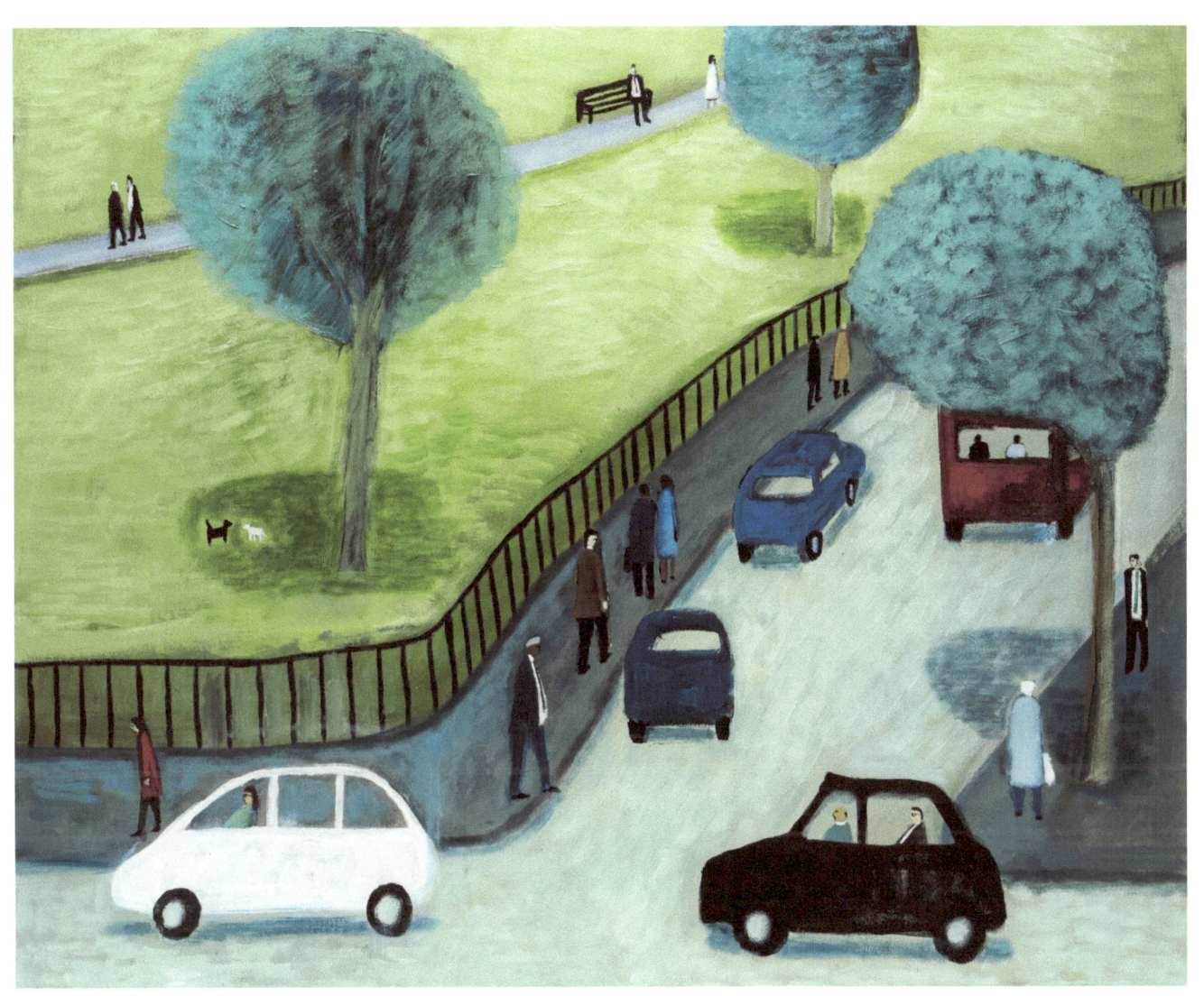

TAXI DRIVER TELLING ME WHAT HE THINKS ABOUT BREXIT, DONALD TRUMP AND ARSENE WENGER

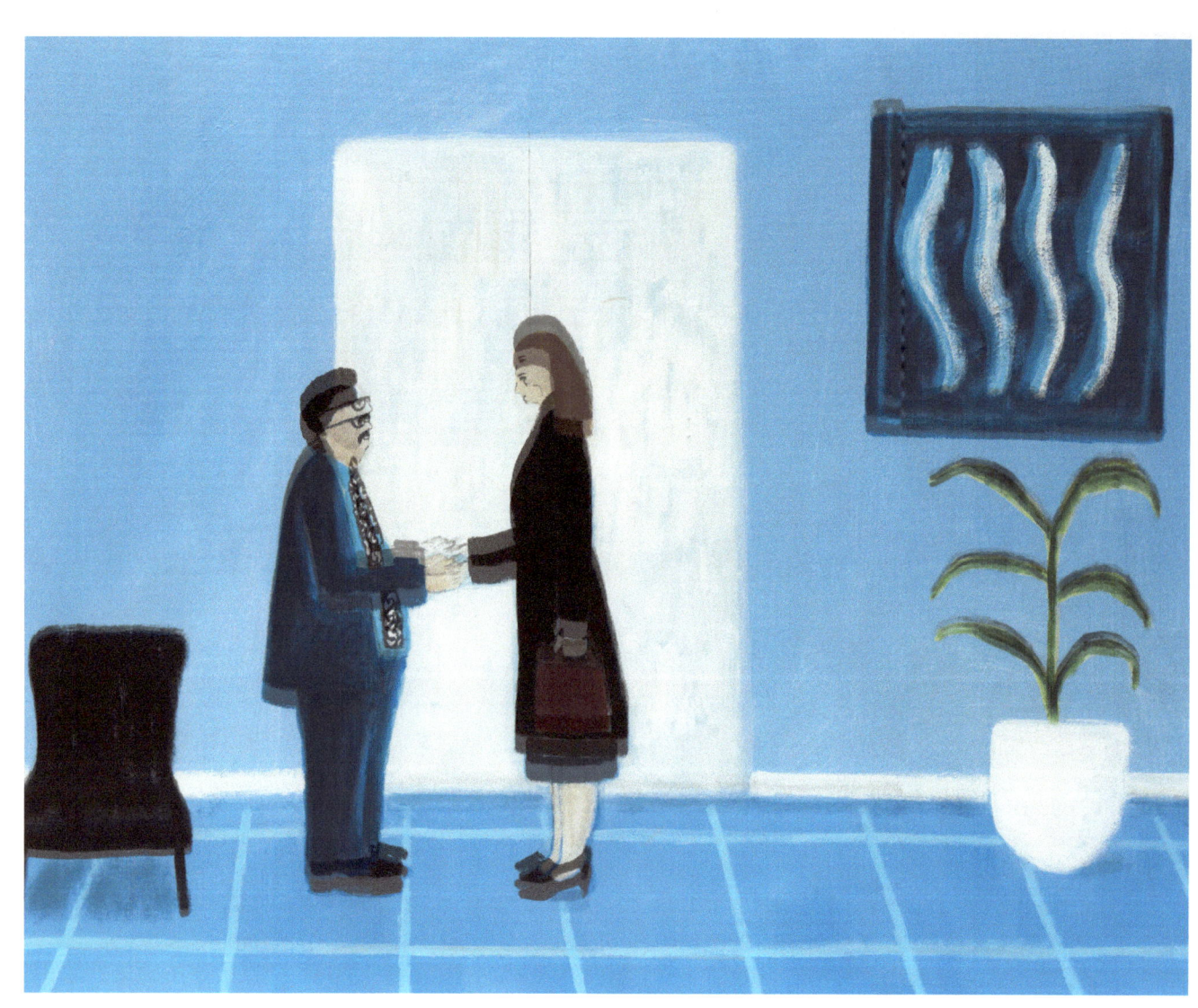

CHARLES TRYING TO BE FLIRTATIOUS

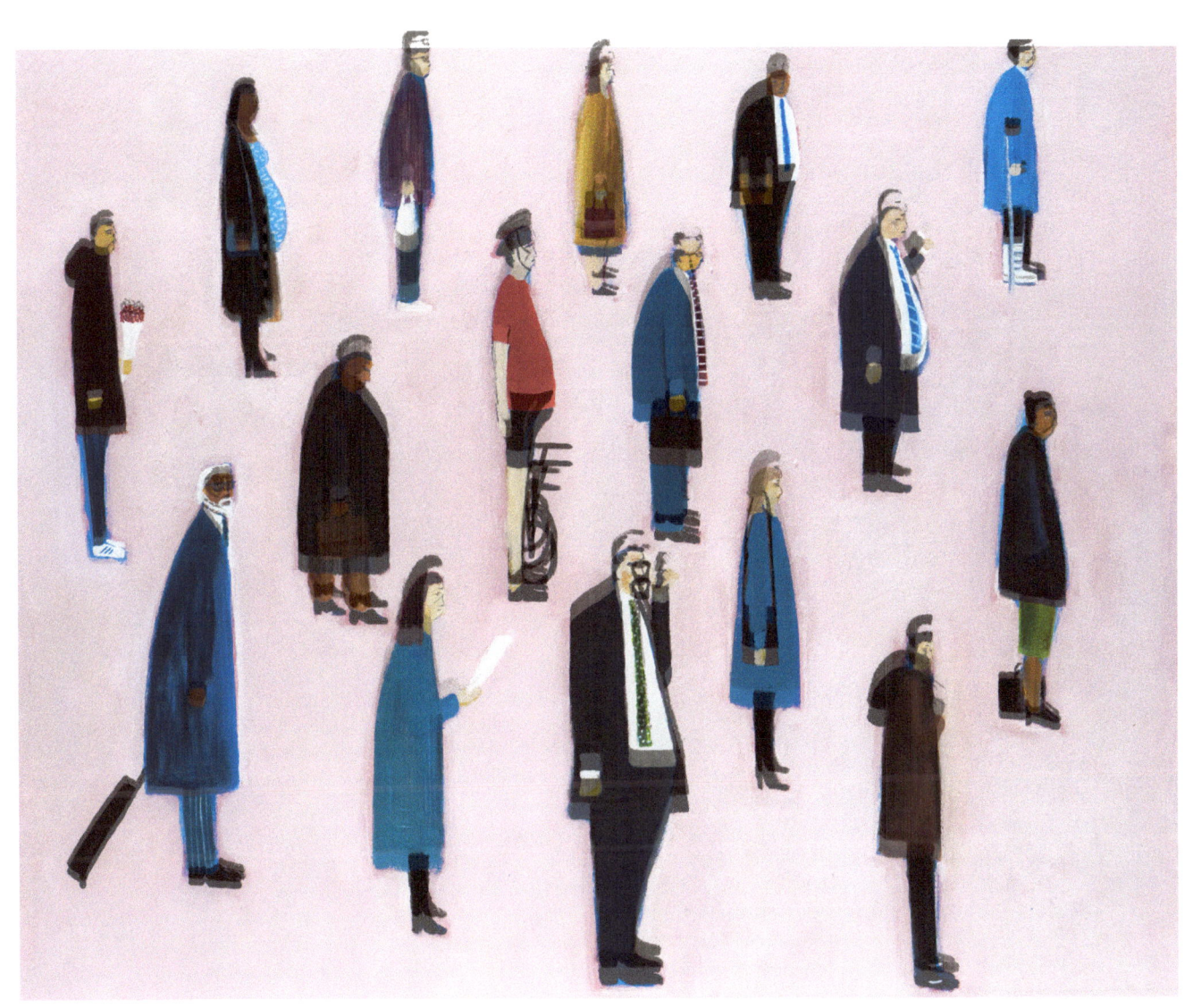

A RANDOM SELECTION OF COMMUTERS

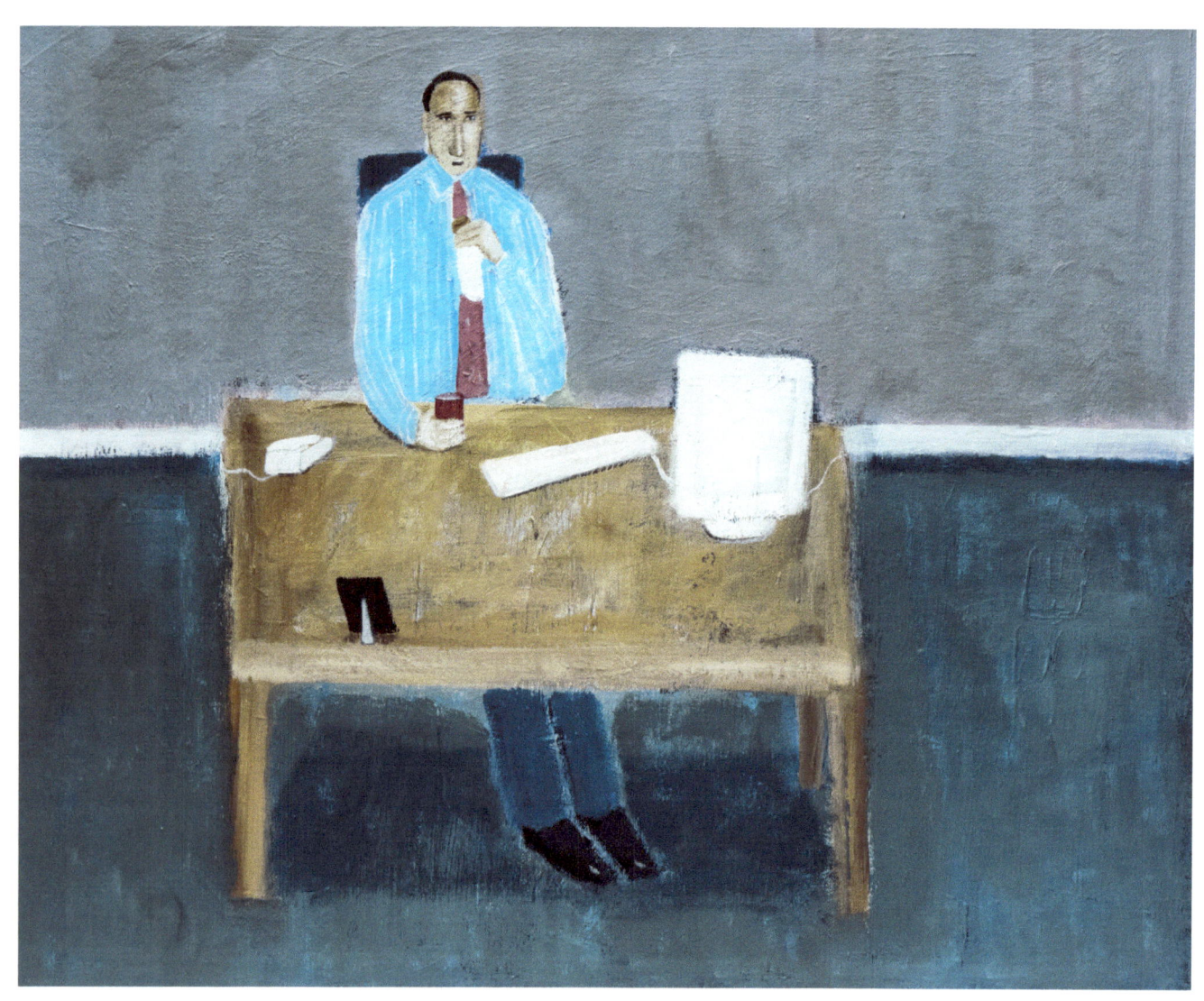

ASSORTED TIE STAINS

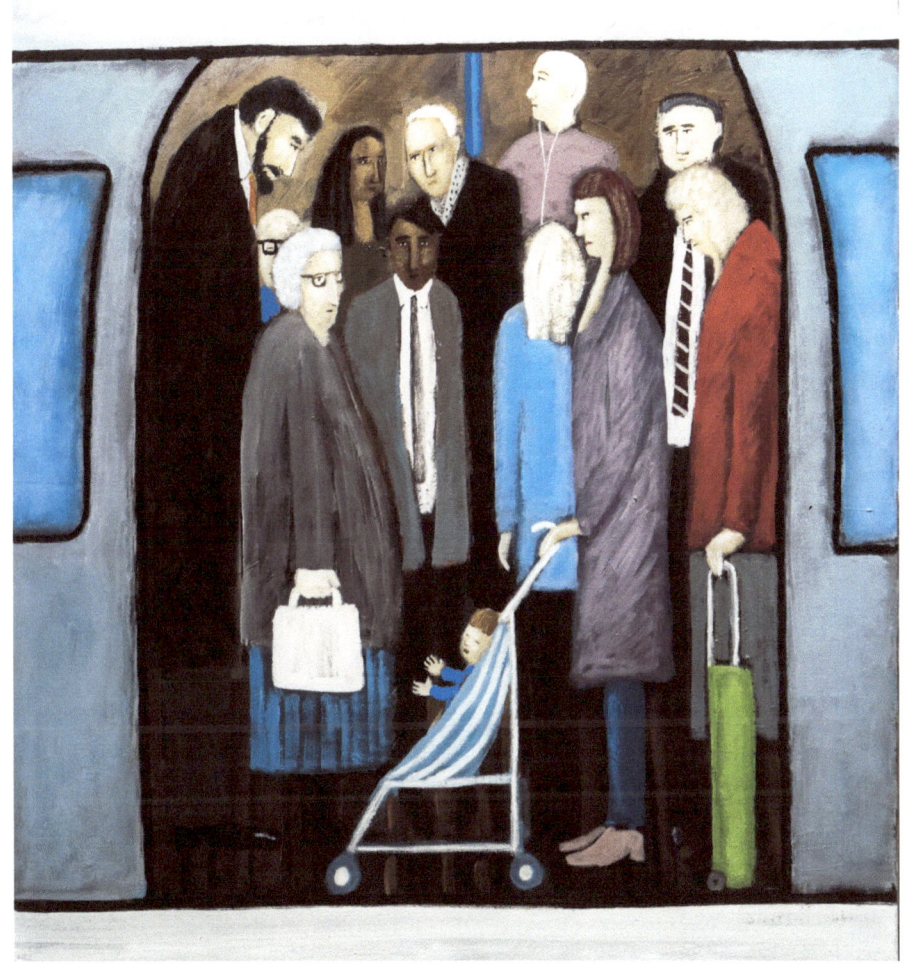

THINKING ABOUT EARLY RETIREMENT

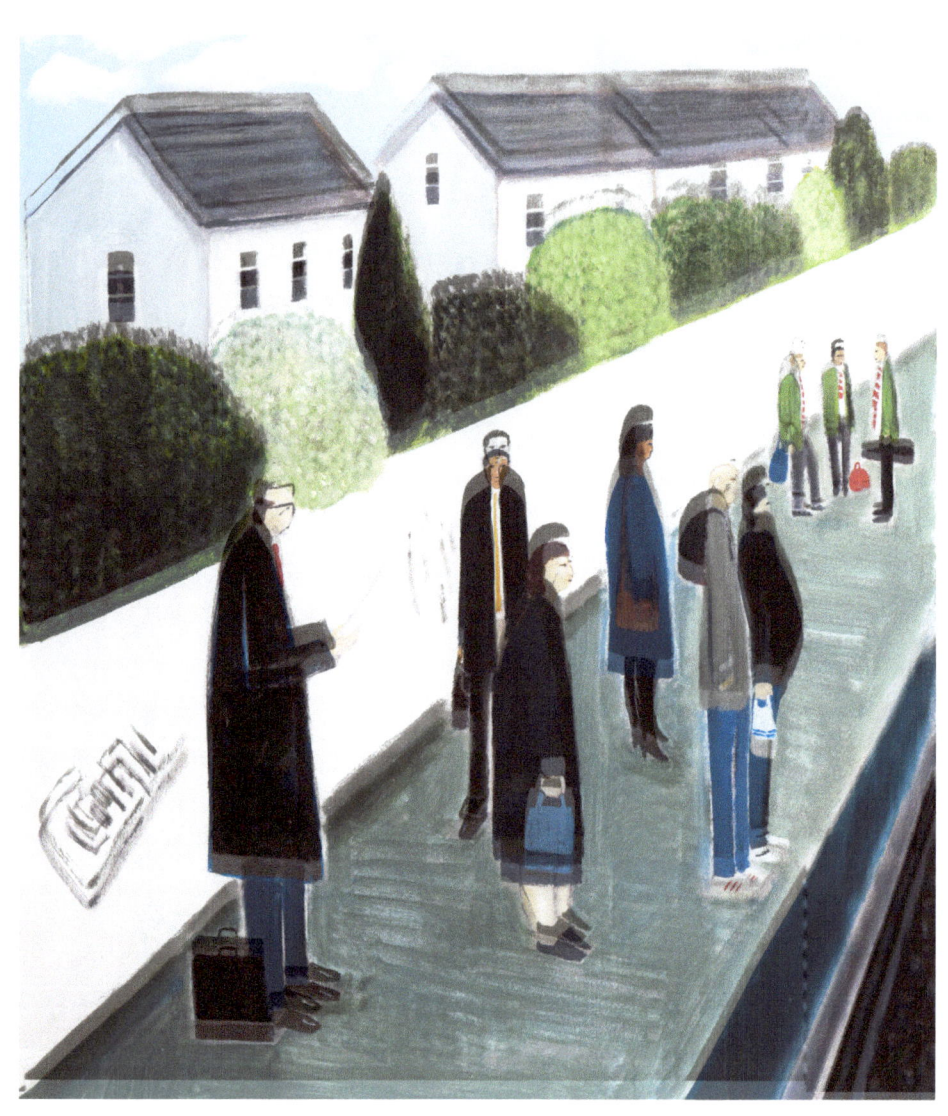

LOUD KIDS ON THE PLATFORM

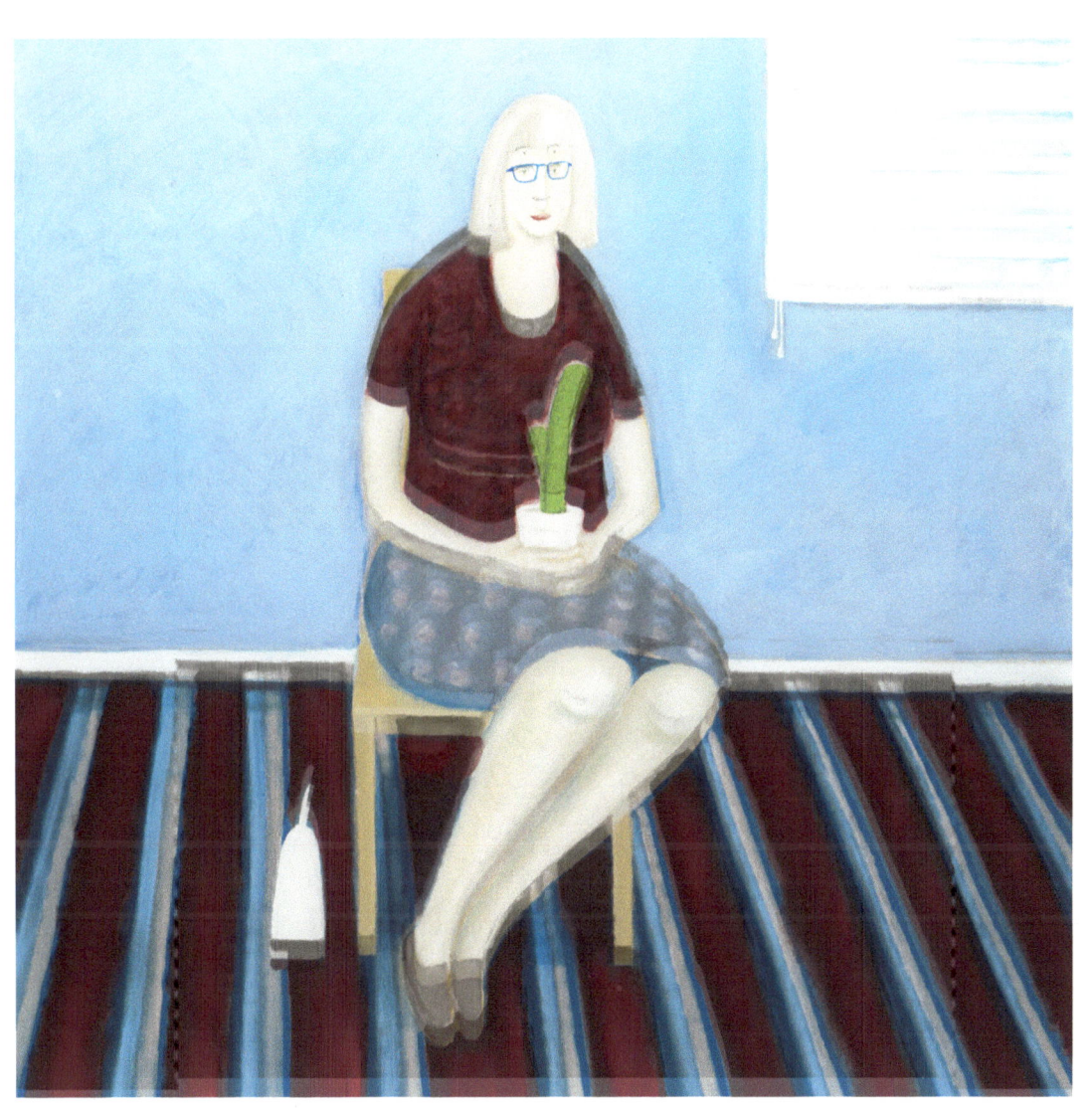

JOYCE WITH HER LEAVING PRESENT

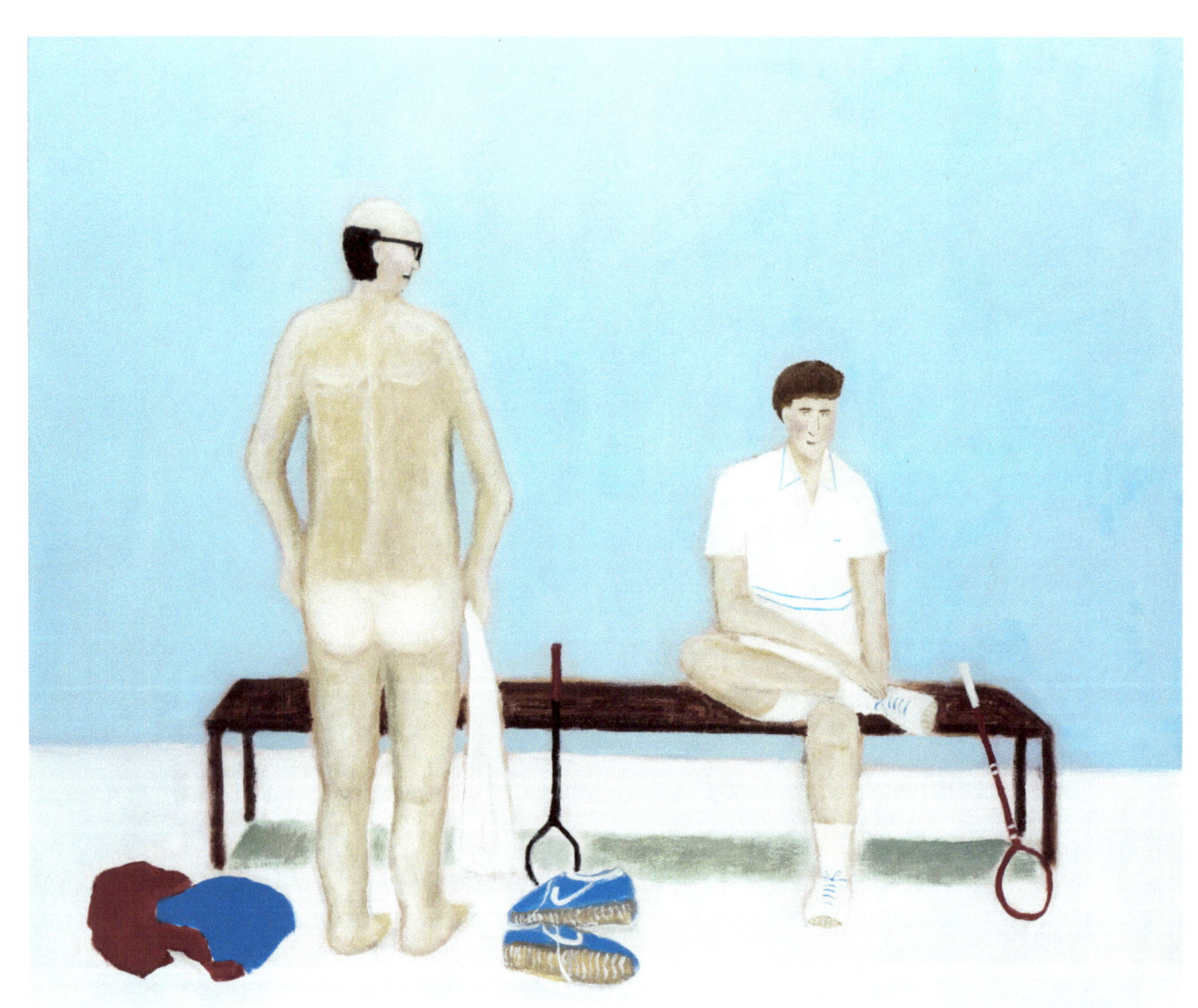

THE CONFIDENT MEMBER

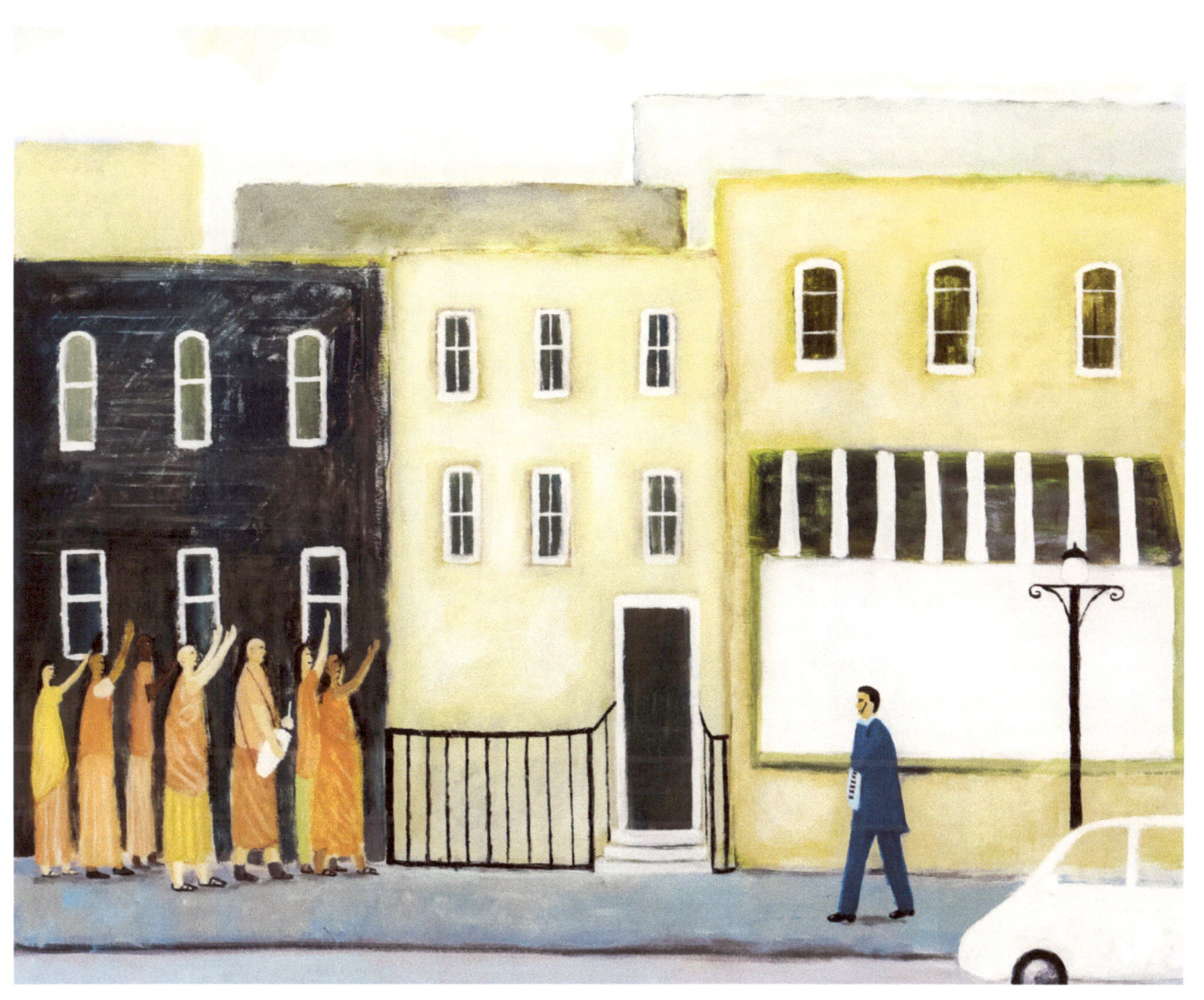

"YOU'LL HAVE TO SPEAK UP JOHN I'M PASSING A LOAD OF HARE KRISHNAS"

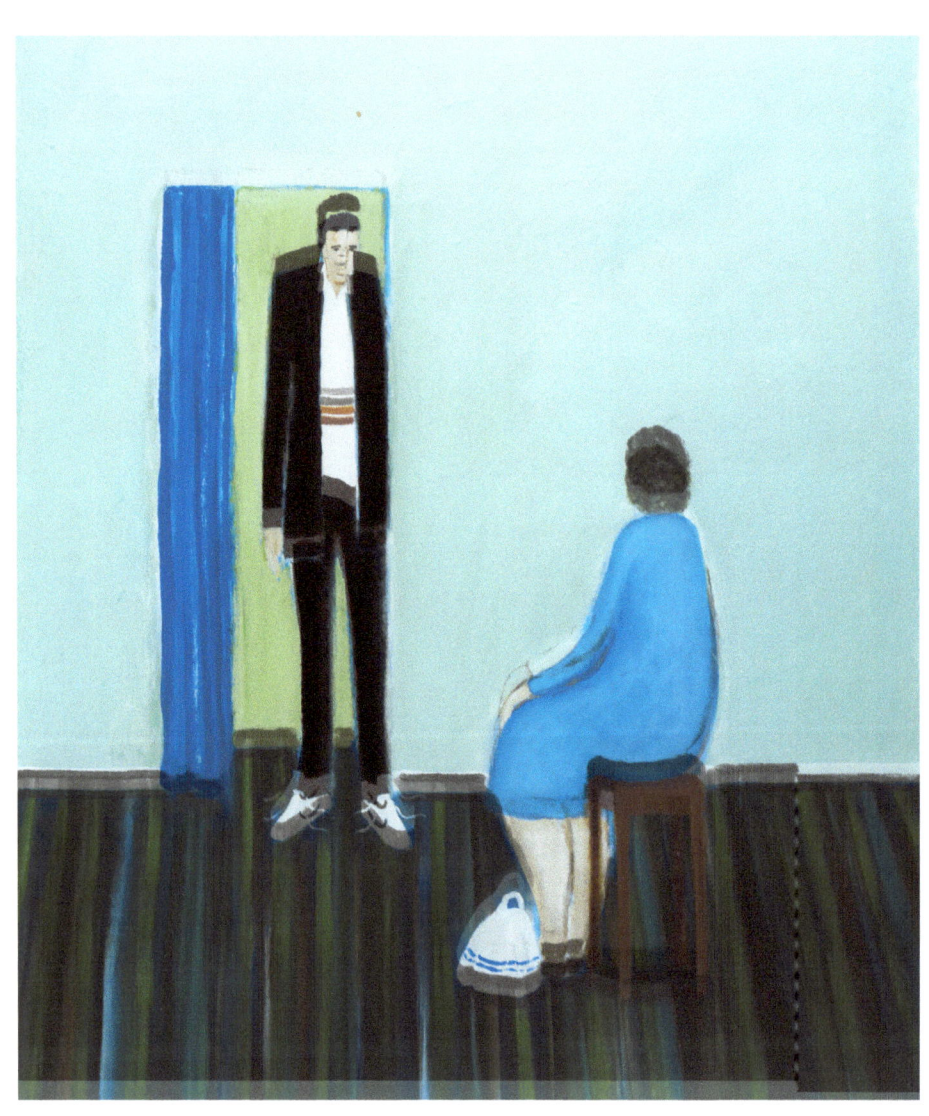

BUYING MY FIRST WORK SUIT WITH MUM

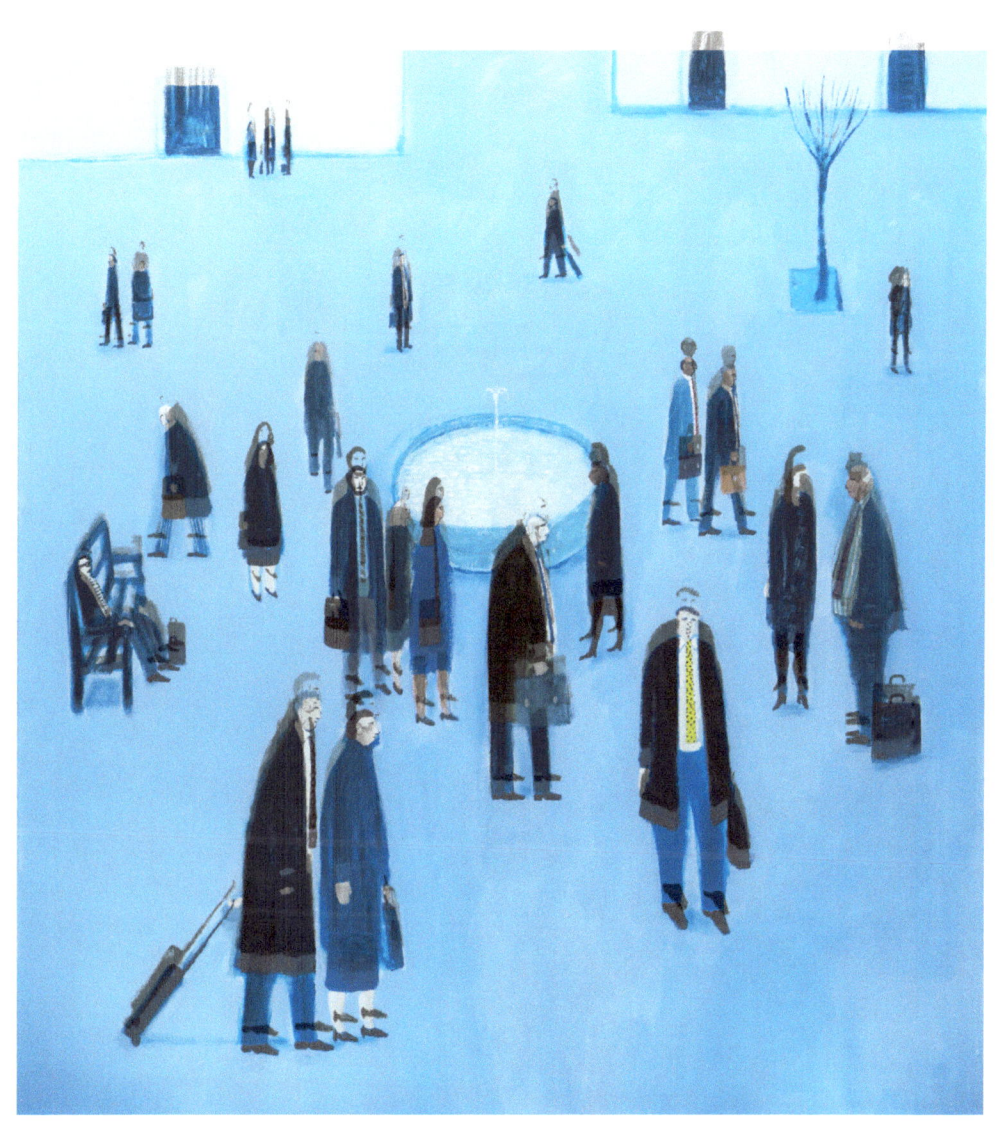

NEW TIE FOR CHRISTMAS

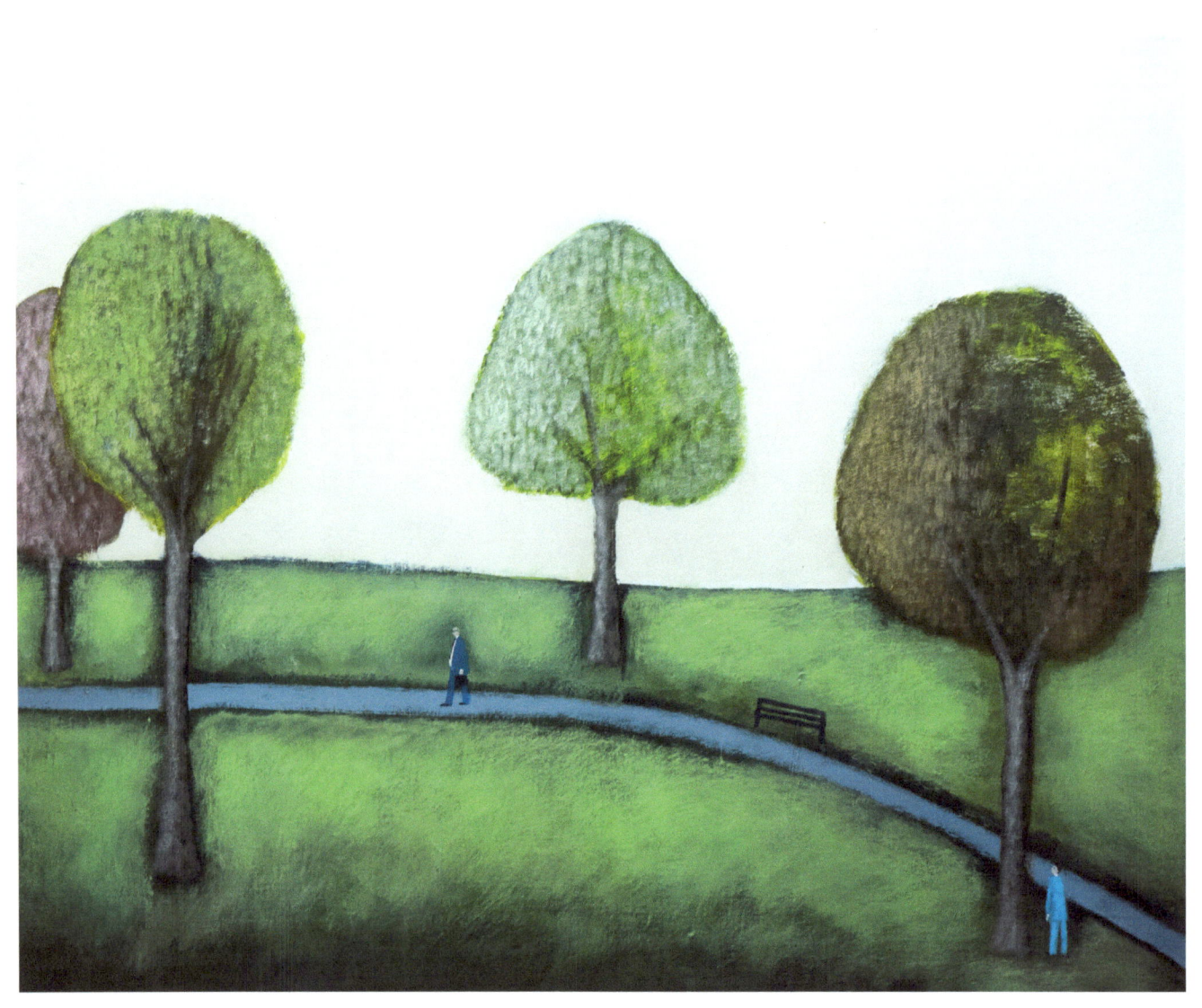
SOMETIMES I'LL HIDE BEHIND A TREE TO AVOID WALKING TO THE STATION WITH BOB

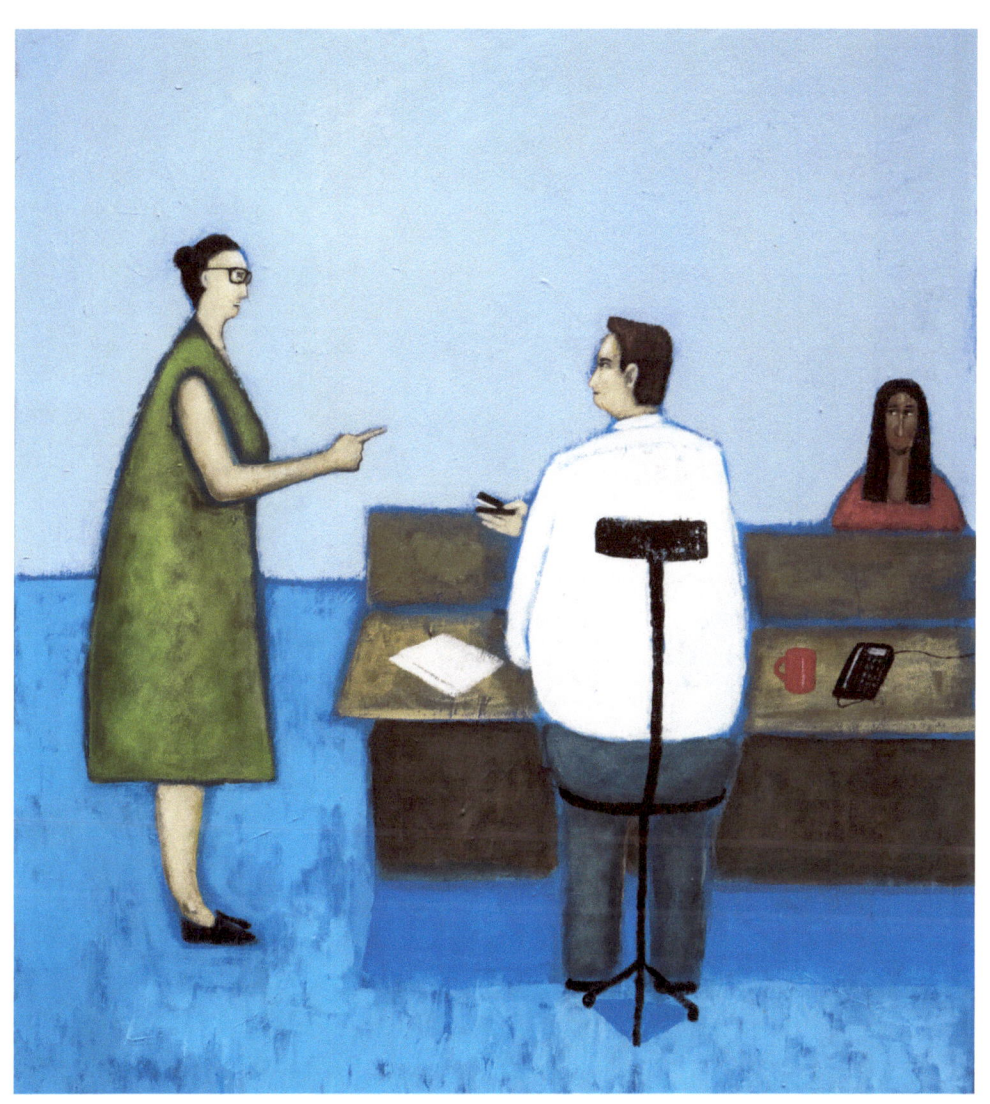

I NEVER TOOK MAUREEN'S STAPLER WITHOUT ASKING AGAIN

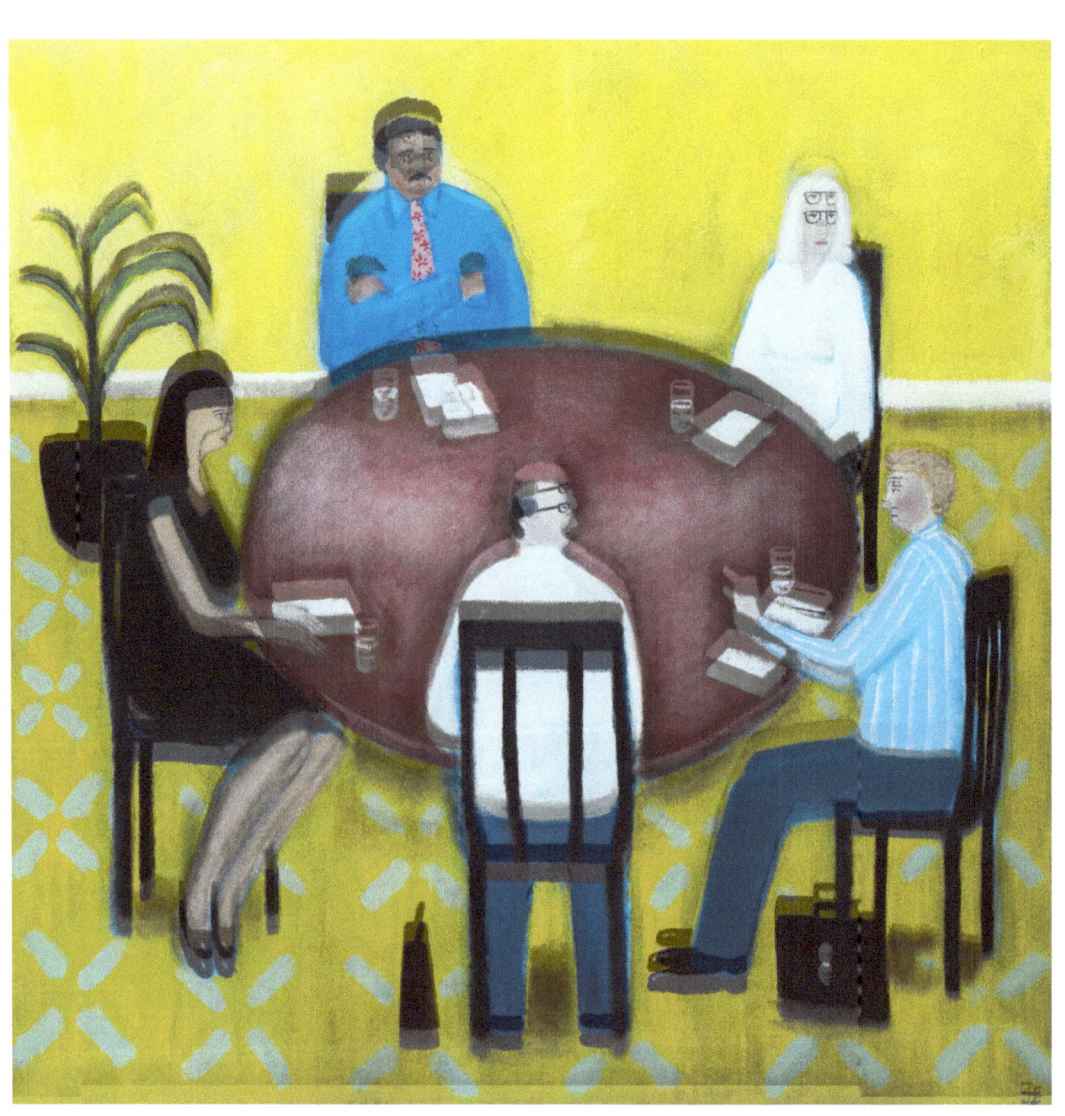

SIMON BEING UNUSUALLY ASSERTIVE

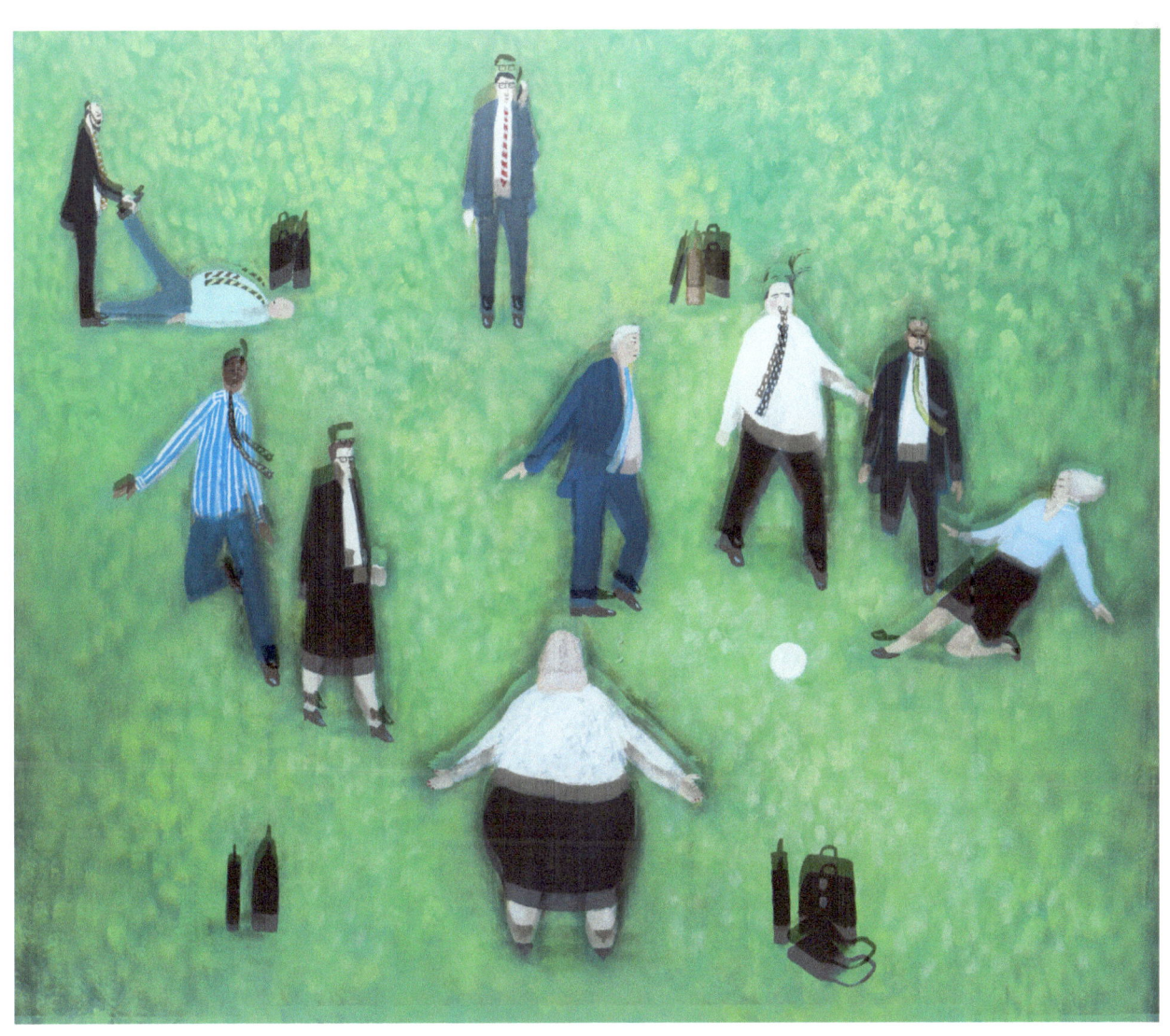

WE OFTEN HAVE A QUICK KICK ABOUT AFTER A BOARD MEETING

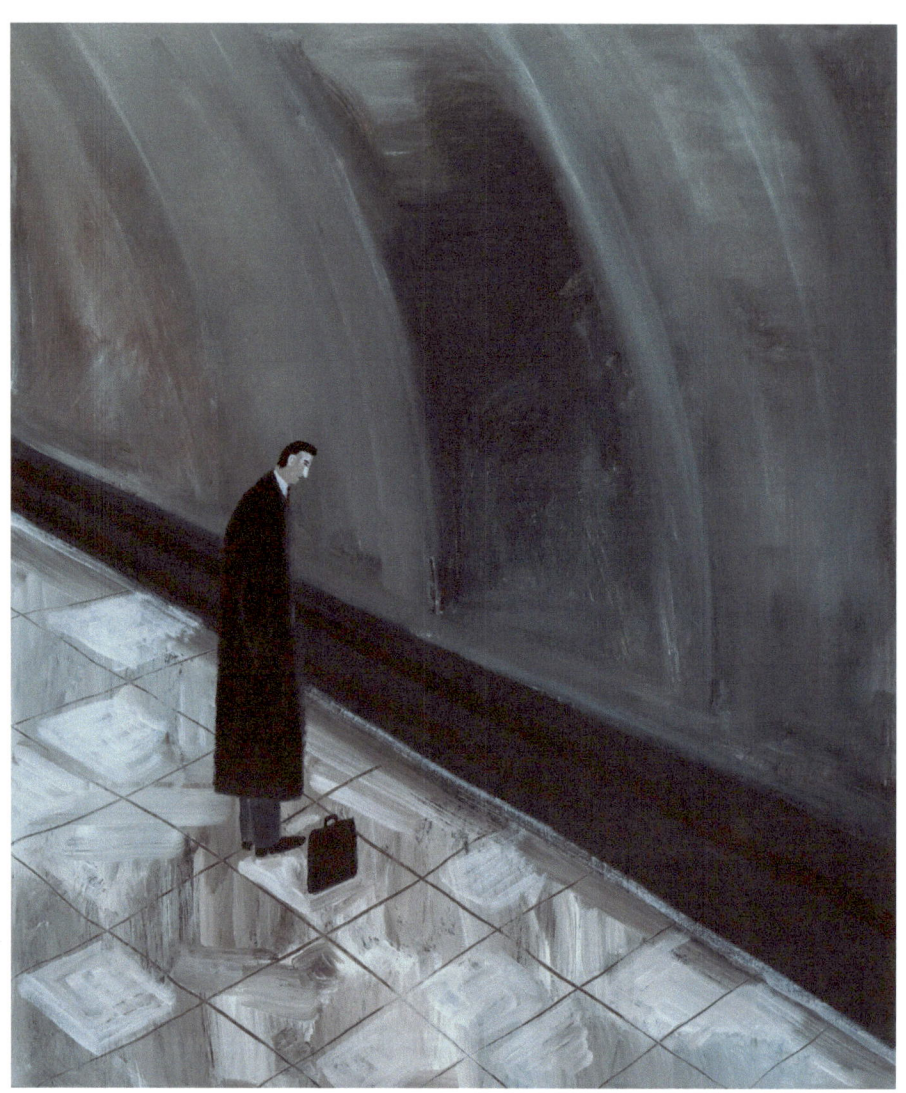

MAN WATCHING A MOUSE

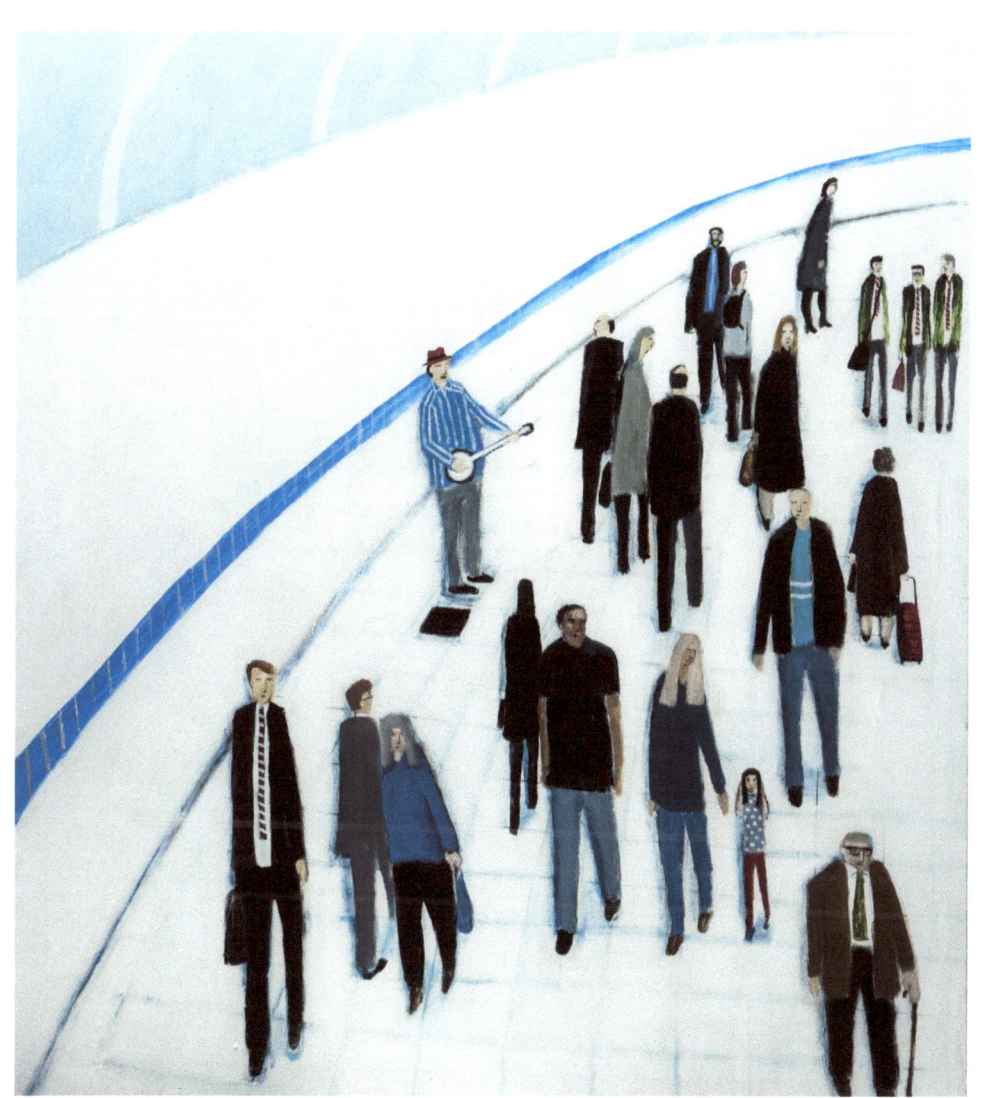

TONE DEAF BUSKER

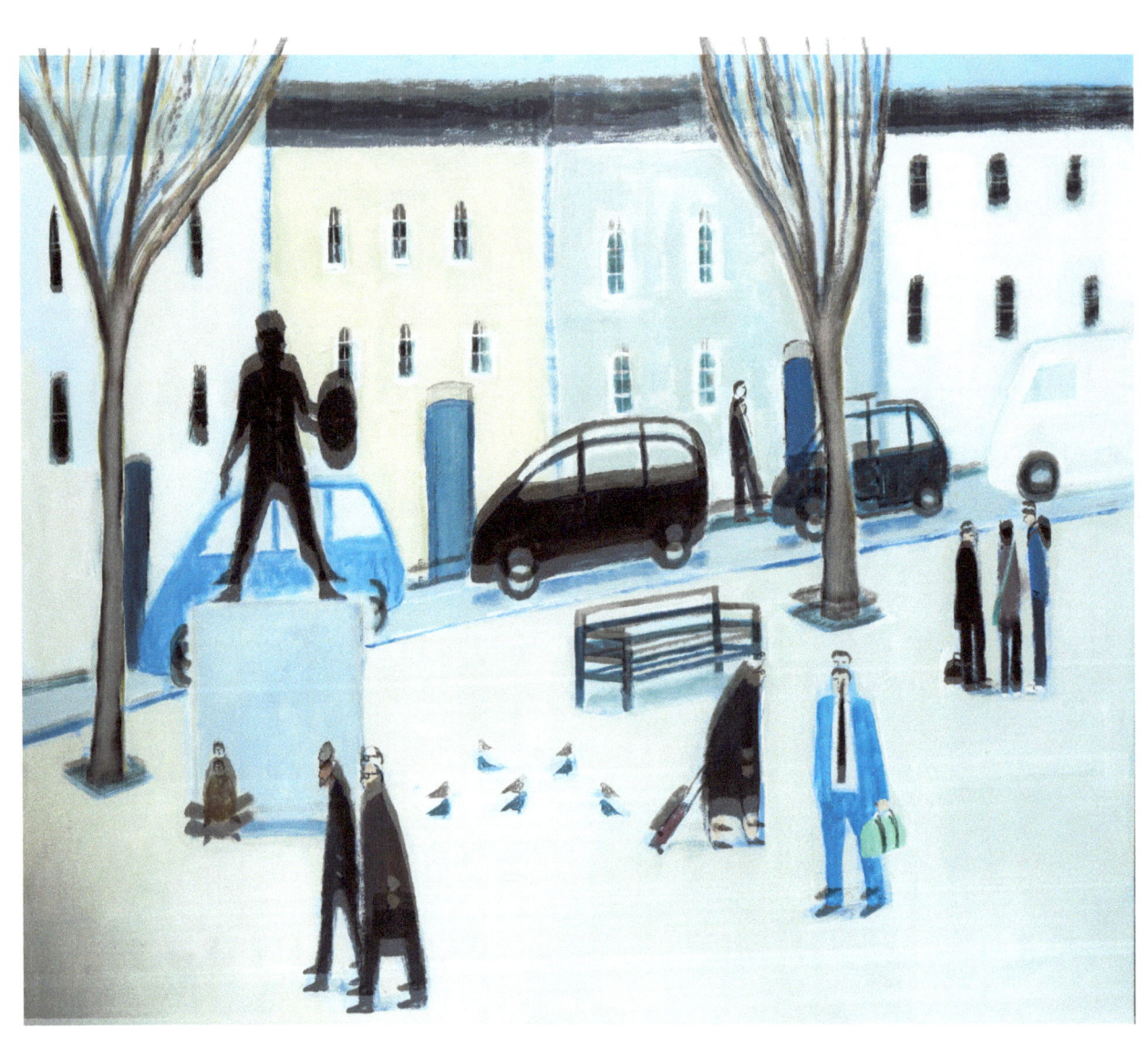

RELUCTANTLY GOING TO THE GYM

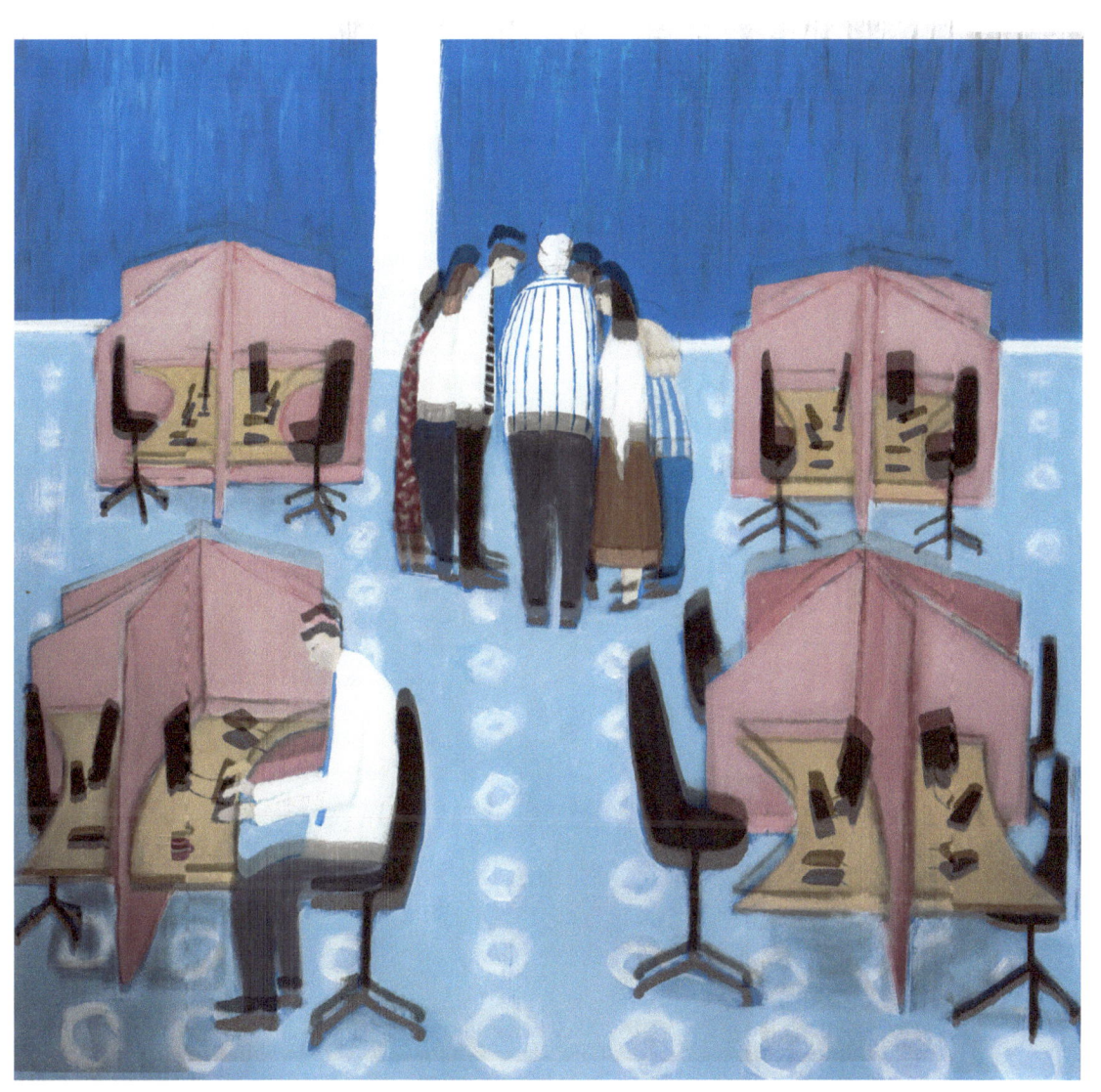

TAKING NO INTEREST IN MAUREEN'S WEDDING PHOTOS

www.ingramcontent.com/pod-product-compliance
Lightning Source LLC
Chambersburg PA
CBHW051927210526
45473CB00006B/2162